This book is very well researched and thought out, clearly articulated and illustrated, and will be especially helpful to those who struggle with reconciling a literal and conservative interpretation of Genesis 1 with what science quite confidently asserts around the age of the universe, earth, living creatures, and the arrival of humanity.

—Pastor Rob McLaren

B.A., B.Ed., M.Div.

A SCIENCE-INFORMED
INTERPRETATION OF THE GENESIS
CREATION WEEK

LET THERE BE *Light*

DAVID S. MACKENZIE

LET THERE BE LIGHT
Copyright © 2024 by David S. MacKenzie

Scriptures taken from the Holy Bible, New International Version®, NIV®. Copyright © 1973, 1978, 1984, 2011 by Biblica, Inc.™ Used by permission of Zondervan. All rights reserved worldwide. www.zondervan.com. The "NIV" and "New International Version" are trademarks registered in the United States Patent and Trademark Office by Biblica, Inc.™ Scripture quotations taken from the (NASB®) New American Standard Bible®, Copyright © 1960, 1971, 1977, 1995, 2020 by The Lockman Foundation. Used by permission. All rights reserved. lockman.org. Scripture quotations are from the ESV® Bible (The Holy Bible, English Standard Version®), © 2001 by Crossway, a publishing ministry of Good News Publishers. Used by permission. All rights reserved. The ESV text may not be quoted in any publication made available to the public by a Creative Commons license. The ESV may not be translated in whole or in part into any other language.

Soft cover ISBN: 978-1-4866-2624-3
Hard cover ISBN: 978-1-4866-2626-7
eBook ISBN: 978-1-4866-2625-0

Word Alive Press
119 De Baets Street Winnipeg, MB R2J 3R9
www.wordalivepress.ca

WORD ALIVE
—P R E S S—

Cataloguing in Publication information can be obtained from Library and Archives Canada.

CONTENTS

ACKNOWLEDGEMENTS

I'D LIKE TO acknowledge my family and many friends who provided encouragement and feedback during the development of this book. In particular, I'd like to thank Ken Boschman for his early enthusiasm regarding my primary thesis.

I also owe a huge debt of gratitude to my editor, Anna-Lisa Ptolemy, who in fact was much more than an editor. She was also a collaborator, friend, and partner as well as my chief critic, in a good way.

Introduction

THE SEARCH FOR ANSWERS

> It is the glory of God to conceal a matter…
> (Proverbs 25:2)

MANY APPROACHES HAVE been taken over the years by scholars, scientists, philosophers, and others in an attempt to interpret the creation account in Genesis. However, I believe that up till now no satisfactory explanation of this narrative has been provided that fully aligns with both science and scripture.

The purpose of this book is to introduce a comprehensive thesis for a new way to harmonize the creation account with the 13.8-billion-year age of the universe and the 4.5 billion years of natural history on the Earth. The counterintuitive explanation being presented here is completely biblical and, to my knowledge, unique. When I say biblical, I mean to say that it's supported by and consistent with all scripture, that it conforms to the structure and message of Genesis, and that it provides a way to read the creation story in a plausibly literal manner. In addition, the biblical principles and structures revealed and highlighted in this book will serve to increase our insight into God's plans and purposes.

Over the course of this analysis, my goal is to establish a framework of thought which allows the words of Genesis to be understood as completely true. This is important because many people seem to have dismissed the biblical testimony about creation as unscientific and implausible. Without a doubt, Genesis has challenged the minds of countless people over the years, and every effort has been made to fully comprehend it. But despite its importance, we know that the creation narrative remains mysterious and somewhat confusing. It is my hope that this book will provide a new perspective and clarity on this subject.

Of course, to believe in God as Creator, it is not necessary to understand all things. We don't need to know every truth, but it's still important to honestly follow all paths which appear to lead to truth. In Romans 1:20 we read, *"For since the creation of the world God's invisible qualities—his eternal power and divine nature—have been clearly seen, being understood from what has been made, so that people are without excuse."* This reminds us that there is reason enough to believe in God and his work regardless of our level of technical knowledge on this subject.

As a reader of this book, you may have had an interest in this subject for many years and know the issues quite well. You may be well-versed in the prevailing theological viewpoints and theories. You may also be familiar with astronomy, geology, paleontology, and anthropology. Or you may be brand new to some of these subjects.

In any case, perhaps take a moment to ask yourself, as a quick mental exercise, what it is you currently believe. Do you ascribe to a literal interpretation of Genesis? Do you reject creationism? Do you believe in an old Earth? Or perhaps you are agnostic and feel it's unknowable. Take note of your beliefs—because after reading this book, you will hopefully have achieved a new level of understanding and insight, no matter where you started.

As we explore this subject, wouldn't it be exciting to uncover fresh truths? How incredible would it be to provide new answers to many age-old questions about the creation narrative and thereby affirm our faith in God and scripture? I love Albert Einstein's view regarding the development of any new thesis:

> ...creating a new theory is not like destroying an old barn and erecting a skyscraper in its place. It is rather like climbing a mountain, gaining new and wider views, discovering unexpected connections between our starting-point and its rich environment.[1]

The Bible itself is a singularly rich environment. Based on patterns discovered within it, I seek to offer a unique perspective on this important topic.

The approach taken in this book—indeed, its inspiration—stems from a belief that God's creation timeline is not haphazard but rather orderly. Based on this conviction, I will introduce a new method for interpreting and understanding the Genesis narrative and its days, called the week-within-a-week creation model. I will demonstrate that it is supported by scripture.

Just as any house needs to be built on firm foundations, any new thesis about Genesis requires the construction of a solid base of biblical precedent, sound reasoning, and scriptural integrity. It needs to stand up to scrutiny before it will be accepted as plausible and valuable.

I will therefore take the time to slowly build such a foundation. This will be done by identifying relevant patterns and cycles in the Bible and establishing important takeaways from these studies. By doing so, I hope to contribute to religious study and demonstrate the trustworthiness of the Bible.

This book contains the important discoveries which form the basis of my thesis. The approach I've taken is a holistic one where the entire Bible, from beginning to end, has relevance.

There is also a prophetic element involved, as some of the ideas in my book are supported by identified prophetic patterns. Through my analysis of these patterns and the associated biblical principles, I seek to show how parts of the Bible are interconnected in new and exciting ways. My hope is that readers will share in the excitement of discovery as this book unravels the enigma that is Genesis.

One

A WAR OF CREDIBILITY

In seeking truth you have to get both sides of the
story.[2] —Walter Cronkite

AS WE BEGIN our quest for a better understanding of the creation narrative, I would like to briefly outline some of its key challenges. Many of you may already be aware of these issues, but I would still like to highlight the reasons I felt it was important to write about this topic.

The central challenge relates to the credibility of both scripture and science. Imagine a court case in which the testimonies provided by two credible witnesses conflict with one another. This situation creates tension for the jury. Either one witness, or both, is lying or mistaken or their testimonies are both true and must somehow be reconciled. As many readers will appreciate, this is the essence of the problem as it relates to the creation narrative when compared to scientific findings.

The Bible in its entirety has tremendous credibility in the minds of people of faith and is considered by believers to be the infallible Word of God. The Bible also testifies about itself and God. Hebrews 6:18 says, *"God did this so that, by two unchangeable things in which it is impossible for God to lie, we who have fled to take hold of the hope set before us may be greatly encouraged."*

David Limbaugh wrote about the reliability of scripture, saying, "Biblical inerrancy was not only affirmed unambiguously by Jesus Christ, but is foundational to our firm reliance on God's promises and revelations contained in the Bible."[3]

We see then that there is a lot riding on the accuracy of Genesis. We also know that Jesus is referred to as the Word of God through whom all things were made (John 1:1–3). Thus, the reliability of Genesis, being the Word of God, can be equated with the credibility of Jesus himself. The stakes could hardly be higher.

On the other side, science also has very high credibility and I dedicate all of Chapter Three to discussing this. Briefly, the quantity and quality of the data, having been amassed from many scientific disciplines over many years, provide indisputable facts about the universe and natural history which cannot be ignored.

This means that wherever there appears to be inconsistency or discrepancy between what scripture and science tell us, there is unresolved tension. This tension can be handled in only so many ways:

- Denying or disputing the findings of science.
- Rejecting the credibility of scripture.
- Watering scripture down to an allegorical or symbolic level.
- Finding different ways to interpret Genesis so it can be understood in a more plausible sense.
- Living with unresolved tension and unknowns.

I believe there are severe drawbacks to the first three options. And if the fourth cannot be achieved, the fifth is also quite unsatisfactory. We will see some of these dynamics at work when we review the different methods of interpretation suggested by theologians in an effort to provide varying degrees of reconciliation.

So what are some of the key areas of conflict to which I have been referring? We find, on the surface, that the Bible and the scientific record appear to give two very different narratives:

BIBLE

- Adam is described as the first man, created about six or seven thousand years ago.
- The fall of Adam (and mankind) is historical and critical.
- The universe and Earth were created in six days.
- God created all things.
- The sun appeared on the fourth day, after the Earth was already in existence.
- There is no mention of evolution. Species reproduce according to their own kind (Genesis 1:12).

SCIENCE

- Anthropology indicates that Homo sapiens existed hundreds of thousands of years ago.
- There is no clear demarcation of a "first" man. The concept of Adam is unproven.
- The universe is measured to be 13.8 billion years old and the Earth 4.5 billion years old.
- Life appeared and evolved over millions of years.
- The Sun was formed about 4.5 billion years ago, before the Earth came into being.
- Lifeforms diversified from a common ancestry over hundreds of millions of years.

In reviewing these authoritative yet seemingly mutually exclusive narratives, we are caught on the horns of a dilemma. Just as it's difficult to reject either narrative as false, it's equally as problematic to accept both as simultaneously true.

And proving both to be true is really what my proposed thesis is all about.

Two

GOD THE CREATOR

> By the word of the Lord the heavens were made,
> their starry host by the breath of his mouth. He
> gathers the waters of the sea into jars; he puts the
> deep into storehouses. (Psalm 33:6–7)

THE GENESIS ACCOUNT of creation is not the only reference in the Bible to God being the Creator of all things. Creation is a central tenet of the Bible, from Genesis to Revelation. Consider the following verses:

> You are worthy, our Lord and God, to receive glory
> and honor and power, for you created all things, and
> by your will they were created and have their being.
> (Revelation 4:11)

> By faith we understand that the universe was formed
> at God's command, so that what is seen was not
> made out of what was visible. (Hebrews 11:3)

> Ah, Sovereign Lord, you have made the heavens
> and the earth by your great power and outstretched
> arm. Nothing is too hard for you. (Jeremiah 32:17)

> Then the angel I had seen standing on the sea and on the land raised his right hand to heaven. And he swore by him who lives for ever and ever, who created the heavens and all that is in them, the earth and all that is in it, and the sea and all that is in it, and said, "There will be no more delay!" (Revelation 10:5–6)

These scriptures represent a small sample of many which declare that God created the universe, the Earth, all living things, and everything else in existence. The entire Bible, including the gospels, and all systematic theology uphold this doctrine.

A plain reading of Genesis conveys clear and unequivocal claims about God's role in creation. A strictly materialistic and evolutionary model of the universe, attributing no creative actions to God, would be inconsistent with biblical testimony. In saying this, I don't claim that evolutionary change and adaptation have not occurred or that evolutionary science is wrong. For the moment, what I am saying is that the testimony of the Bible would be contradicted if there was no supernatural, intentional, and purposeful creation by God of all things.

The Apostles' Creed confesses, "I believe in one God, the Father almighty, creator of heaven and earth."[4] Accordingly, if everything in the universe is a product of undirected material formation and random chance, the creation narrative—indeed, the entire Bible—would need to be considered merely allegorical at best and an outright fabrication at worst.

In summary, any theory about Genesis which does not acknowledge and affirm that God is the Creator would be inconsistent with scripture.

The Bible's declaration isn't just that God created all things but also that his character is revealed through creation. For example, Psalm 19:1 says, *"The heavens declare the glory of God; the skies proclaim the work of his hands. Day after day they pour forth speech;*

night after night they reveal knowledge." And in Isaiah 46:10 we read, "*I make known the end from the beginning, from ancient times, what is still to come.*" Here we are told that God reveals his plans. Then Isaiah 40:26 says,

> Lift up your eyes and look to the heavens: who created all these? He who brings out the starry host one by one and calls forth each of them by name. Because of his great power and mighty strength, not one of them is missing.

This passage confirms God's personal relationship and involvement with his creation. Rather than being remote and impersonal, he knows and loves all his created things.

These scriptural understandings about God are central to my thesis as I seek to provide a full reconciliation between science and Genesis.

In summary, the basis of this book is to respect and accept biblical testimony regarding God as Creator. Indeed, this confidence in scripture has inspired me to seek a viable explanation of the Genesis narrative that can be harmonized with all the evidence of science. The answers to this challenge and mystery have long eluded discovery.

Three

THE SCIENTIFIC METHOD

> The scientific method, I think, is the highest
> philosophical height that mankind has ever
> produced. It seeks constantly to disprove itself.
> What other philosophy is there that does that?[5]
> —Christopher Nolan

THE SCIENTIFIC METHOD is a systematic and objective process by which explanations for observed natural phenomena can be identified and confirmed. It was developed in the sixteenth and seventeenth centuries by Francis Bacon and René Descartes as a methodical approach to understanding how matter and energy in the natural world operate and relate to each other.[6]

It was designed to remove a scientist's personal bias or preconceived ideas by forcing them to focus on empirical data derived from observation, measurement, and testing, and then to form various hypotheses to provide a full explanation for what has been observed. These hypotheses are then subject to testing and, if they stand up well, can be used to make predictions about the results of new experiments or observations.

This methodology has been of enormous benefit to mankind and has led to the advancement of knowledge and technology at an accelerating speed. As an approach to learning and discovering facts about physical processes in the universe and the natural world, it's indispensable.

Measurements and observations are mostly objective in nature and generally more certain than theories. For example, if you measure the speed of several golf balls hit by five different golf pros, the measured speeds are not subject to debate. The speeds are what they are. On the other hand, when golf analysts or physics professors develop theories as to the why and how of different swings and distances, many factors are involved. The resulting theories may include differences in mental approaches, swing mechanics, strength, talent, nervous system variations, varying swing paths, speed, and direction of ball spin.

As you can see, measurement and outcomes are more easily identified and quantified than causes. This relates to the thesis of this book. Just as it's easier to determine the speed of a golf ball rather than why each golfer swings the way they do, we can easily observe how the universe and natural world operate, but it's far more difficult to understand their ultimate first causes, complex interactions, or meaning.

In science, better technologies are constantly being developed to provide more accurate measurements. As these measurements are refined, they affect current theories. Sometimes completely new data is suddenly discovered, new fossils are found, or new observations about the universe are made, such as those being supplied by the powerful James Webb telescope.[7]

In such cases, all new information needs to be incorporated and explained by existing theories in order for those theories to remain viable.

Einstein was once shown a newspaper which claimed, "One hundred German scientists claim Einstein's Theory of Relativity is wrong," to which Einstein supposedly replied, "If I were wrong, then one would have been enough!"[8]

Two important points can be gleaned from this anecdote.

First, for a theory to be useful it must be falsifiable. If a theory's prediction fails, it's either a failed theory or one that needs amendment.

Second, science isn't ultimately maintained by consensus but rather by the development of theories which stand up to repeated testing. New theories are continually being developed to explain observed phenomena. Often one theory is found to be better than others at doing so, and generally this is the theory that will be adopted.

Occam's razor applies here: everything should be kept as simple as possible, but no simpler. And of course all theories are subject to continual testing and scrutiny based on new observational or experimental data that becomes available.

The confidence level of existing measurements and scientific findings is proportional to the quantity and quality of the data available, which includes all the observations, measurements, and testing that have been completed. In the fields of astronomy, paleontology, and anthropology, the total amount of evidence that has been amassed is staggering and irrefutable. For this reason, any attempt to reconcile scripture with science requires a thesis that accepts and incorporates all the findings of science within it.

I would like to note that the scientific method does have limitations in the pursuit of truth. For example, science cannot prove or disprove God. Nor can it infuse meaning into life. Science is also incapable of making value judgments or aesthetic distinctions. It doesn't draw conclusions from supernatural phenomena nor determine how scientific knowledge should be used. Huston Smith made this statement:

> The scientific method is nearly perfect for under-
> standing the physical aspects of our life. But it is
> a radically limited viewfinder in its inability to offer
> values, morals and meaning that are at the centre
> of our lives.[9]

Other weaknesses in the scientific method warrant mention. Its findings can be influenced by human bias in interpreting data and can be prejudiced due to conditions where politics or funding of research apply pressure to deliver "acceptable" results.[10]

In this vein Jacob Brownowski warned, "No science is immune to the infection of politics and the corruption of power."[11]

Overall, however, science does its thing extremely well.

Human existence means being exposed to a wide variety of experiences, senses, emotions, and intuitions. For example, life is filled with the need to judge the morality of all kinds of human activity and thought, including our own. These judgments as to what is good, bad, and evil are real and important. They're also outside and beyond the scope of science.

Let me show you what I mean, and perhaps date myself in the process! At one point in my university career, I studied philosophy and psychology at the same time. In philosophy we debated free will versus determinism, and in psychology we read B.F. Skinner's book, *Beyond Freedom and Dignity*,[12] which promotes the idea of using technology to control human behaviour and thus override free choice. I was therefore studying much the same topic in both courses but from different perspectives.

The philosophical argument for causal determinism is that the decisions a person makes are not their own but rather the product of antecedent conditions such as heredity, environment, family history, social conditioning, biological processes, and many other factors which are outside the control of the individual.[13]

According to this argument, every "choice" an individual makes is basically already "baked in the cake"—or, in other words, predetermined. The choice isn't free at all but only appears to be so.

Predeterminism presents an interpretation of the universe where all actions and reactions are driven by the impersonal and rigid laws of physics, chemistry, and biology and one process invariably and mechanically leads to the next. In such a universe, there is no need for God and no place for freedom. Indeed, one could ask at what point in the process real freedom could inject itself into the biological and mental processes of humanity if all that came before was predetermined.

In some ways, a deterministic perspective is logical and can be easily defended, because the universe is defined by cause-and-effect relationships. On the other hand, this strictly mechanical picture of the universe does not correspond with how we actually live our lives, nor with what we really believe about ourselves and others. As humans, we hold ourselves and each other responsible for the choices we make and invariably ascribe moral judgments upon them. Most people think and act as though their lives have meaning and significance, which would be difficult to justify if we actually had no choices in life at all.

In this regard, the theory of predeterminism does not seem to stand up to the tests that real life presents. In addition, it contradicts scripture. The Bible teaches that man has free will and can make his own choices, and indeed that those choices are laden with significant moral consequences. Joshua 24:15 says,

> But if serving the Lord seems undesirable to you, then choose for yourselves this day whom you will serve, whether the gods your ancestors served beyond the Euphrates, or the gods of the Amorites, in whose land you are living. But as for me and my household, we will serve the Lord.

This discussion about choice and free will is relevant in that it highlights the distinction between science's ability to identify antecedent conditions—such as heredity, environment, biological, and psychological factors—and its inability to completely explain the phenomenon of free choice.

The hypothesis of God's existence, while not provable scientifically, does provide a framework of understanding that matches our experiences and observations. This principle, I believe, may also be relevant to any thesis on origins: science can observe and measure most aspects of the mechanics controlling the universe, but it cannot reveal first causes or the reason why the universe exists.

We find in the Bible the answers to many questions about human life that cannot be addressed by science. Science does not attempt to provide answers that cannot be found using physical evidence. But that doesn't mean humans don't seek answers about these issues anyway. If science is of no help to us concerning the spiritual aspects of life, we must look elsewhere.

In turn, the Bible isn't helpful to science in determining such things as the value of the scientific measurement of the Hubble constant. In essence, the paths of religion and science are divergent. Both routes have strengths and both have weaknesses. As Einstein once remarked, "Science without religion is lame, religion without science is blind."[14] They each take a different road to discover truth, but that does not mean that both paths do not ultimately lead to the same destination. In contrast to science, the Bible provides a clear explanation as to where the eternal soul of humanity came from, how we were imbued with free will, why concerns about morality dominate our lives, and many other pressing questions in life.

Although religion and science are different, it's possible to use the scientific method to test the accuracy of certain aspects of scripture. For example, we can test the archaeological and scientific claims of the Bible.

With respect to this book, I will present an opportunity to compare the timetable of the Genesis model to that of the natural history of the universe and life. If these timelines match, my theory will provide additional evidence that the Bible is a trustworthy source of information about our world and therefore also about God.

Psalm 34:8 says, *"Taste and see that the Lord is good."* This is an invitation to test the hypothesis that there is a God and that he is good.

Recall Matthew 22:21 when Jesus told the Pharisees, *"Then render to Caesar the things that are Caesar's; and to God the things that are God's."*

In the same way, there is a case to be made that we should, in the honest pursuit of truth, render unto science the things that are science and to God the things that are God's. The chapters that follow are my honest attempt to do just that.

Four

WHAT IS A DAY?

But if you cannot understand how [creation] could have been done in six days, then grant the Holy Spirit the honor of being more learned than you are.[15] —Martin Luther

THE GENESIS NARRATIVE is presented in the form of a creation week. Its author tells us that this week consisted of six creation days plus a sabbath day when God rested from his work. A central question for any analysis of Genesis is this: why would God choose to communicate his creation using this particular time structure? It seems important to determine the full meaning and implications of this pattern to establish a correct understanding of the whole creation narrative.

Many approaches have been taken to address the question of what is meant by the use of the word "day." The explanations display varying degrees of merit and shortcomings. The focus of this book is to present what I believe to be a unique and better way to explain the days of Genesis.

For biblical literalists, there has always been a strong inclination to consider the days of Genesis to be actual twenty-four-hour days. The advent of modern science has made this position quite difficult to defend, but it is still fiercely held by many people. And while it appears easy for some to dismiss such an unscientific position, doing so quickly and without thought can lead us to discard the underlying importance of the many specific scriptural references to the days of creation.

So, in the interest of gaining a better understanding, let's review the scriptural basis for maintaining that the word "day" has profound significance.

As one example, Dr. Stephen Boyd completed statistical analyses of Genesis 1:1–23 based on the use of Hebrew text, morphology, syntax, verb usage, and vocabulary to determine whether the Genesis narrative is poetry, prose, or a concise report of actual events.[16]

In his study, he used a statistically valid, stratified random sample of forty-eight narrative and forty-nine poetry texts generated from all the narrative and poetry texts in the Bible. He then subjected them to statistical tests. He compared verb usage from four historical events described in the Bible to counterpart poetic descriptions of the same events found elsewhere in the Bible. Using logistic regression, he calculated the probability that Genesis 1:1–23 is an actual narrative to be 0.9999972604. Statistically speaking, it's a virtual certainty.

This study has three major implications:

1. It is not statistically defensible to read Genesis 1:1–23 as poetry.
2. If Genesis 1:1–23 is a narrative, it should be read the same way other Hebrew narratives are intended to be read: as a concise report of actual events used to convey an unmistakable theological message.
3. When this text is read as a narrative, there is only one tenable view of its plain sense: God created everything in six days.

Exodus 20:11 further confirms the meaning of the days in the creation narrative. The fourth of the Ten Commandments instructs the Israelites to work for six days and rest for one. God said, *"For in six days the Lord made the heavens and the earth, the sea, and all that is in them, but he rested on the seventh day."*

There are two key takeaways from this passage. One is that the six days of God's creation program have profound significance. Secondly, the six days plus the creation sabbath day presented a prototype of the sabbath week God prescribed to the Israelites.

The Hebrew week is a cycle of seven days, mirroring the seven-day creation week. Emphasizing this relationship, the names of the days of the Hebrew week are simply each day's number within the week.[17] For example, the week begins with Day One (Yom Rishon) on Sunday and ends with Saturday on Day Seven (Yom Shabbat).

There are other reasons to take the use of the word "day" seriously. "Day," in combination with an associated number, occurs 357 times outside of the Genesis creation narrative. On almost all these occasions, it relates to a twenty-four-hour period.

For example, Exodus 24:16 reads, *"And the glory of the Lord settled on Mount Sinai. For six days the cloud covered the mountain, and on the seventh day the Lord called to Moses from within the cloud."*

We will further discuss this pattern of numbered days in Chapter Fourteen.

Throughout the creation narrative, we read a repeated phrase: "There was evening and there was morning." This description seems to reinforce the argument for typical days and nights.

These biblical references strongly support the idea that the use of the word "day" has real significance. The Genesis structure of a week with seven days is suggestive of a non-random creation process within a specific division of time. For these reasons, the traditional interpretation has always been to consider the days of Genesis as typical days of twenty-four-hour periods.

Due to modern scientific discoveries regarding the age of the universe and the Earth itself, however, many people dismiss this interpretation. That doesn't mean the use of the word "day" in Genesis doesn't still have profound meaning, or that it's irrelevant to understanding the creation narrative.

Those who don't believe in literal twenty-four-hour creation days interpret them in several different ways, including considering the days to be poetic, as language used to convey general truths about creation, or simply as long periods of time. However, such approaches seem to dilute the significance of the word "day" and risk dismissing some of the important meaning associated with it.

Therefore, a crucial question arises: can a new framework be developed that retains the apparent intended meaning of "day" in scripture and also aligns itself with science? This is the question we will put to the test. We will require that any acceptable theory explaining the Genesis account provide a plausible explanation for the days of creation.

Five

SEVEN, THE NUMBER OF PERFECTION

> All the words of the Lord are flawless, like silver
> purified in a crucible, like gold refined seven times.
> (Psalm 12:6)

THE BIBLE CONTAINS more than seven hundred references to the number seven.[18] In biblical numerology, seven symbolizes completion or perfection. In ancient Near Eastern and Israelite culture and literature, it communicated a sense of fullness.[19] This means that when seven, or multiples of seven, appear in the Bible, the intent is to communicate more than just a number: the use of the number seven confirms the completion of the process or purpose of God.

In this book, I focus on several patterns and cycles which revolve around this number to help us more fully understand the Genesis narrative and focus on the significance of the number seven and its biblical meanings. I also believe that the use of the number seven is more than symbolic, and that any events associated with it really do involve that number.

For example, Jesus performed seven healing miracles on the sabbath, which is the seventh day of the week (Mark 1:21–31, 3:1–6, Luke 13:10–17, 14:1–6, John 9:1–6). In order for Jesus's actions on the sabbath to truly convey the idea of perfect healing, rest, and complete health, there had to have been seven actual healings.

Consider these additional examples of the use of seven in the Bible.

In the book of Joshua, we read about the battle of Jericho. It was at Jericho that the Israelites experienced their first victory in the Promised Land. In Joshua 6:3–4, God orders Joshua,

> March around the city once with all the armed men. Do this for six days. Have seven priests carry trumpets of rams' horns in front of the ark. On the seventh day, march around the city seven times, with the priests blowing the trumpets.

This is a seven-day pattern, with seven revolutions around the city on the seventh day. This multiplier effect is associated with a demonstration of God's power and victory, as the walls of Jericho came tumbling down and the Israelites were given a historic victory. This victory foreshadowed the many military successes of the Israelites and their ultimate possession of the Promised Land.

The book of Revelation includes fifty-five uses of the number seven and five uses of the word seventh. There are seven churches, letters, spirits, golden lampstands, stars, seals, horns, eyes, angels, trumpets, thunders, heads, crowns, plagues, golden bowls, hills, and kings. These all point to the complete judgment of God under the perfect Lordship of Christ.[20]

In Chapter Twelve, we will review Daniel's prophecy of seventy weeks. Daniel 9:24 announces, *"Seventy 'sevens' are decreed for your people and your holy city..."* We will see that this prophecy refers to seventy times seven years, or 490 years. Rabbi Jason Sobel states, "490 is the numerical value of the biblical word *tamim* which means to 'complete,' 'perfect,' or 'finished.'"[21]

This multiples-of-seven format is also used to describe perfect forgiveness. In Matthew 18:21–22, we read,

> Then Peter came up and said to Him, "Lord, how many times shall my brother sin against me and I still forgive him? Up to seven times?"
>
> Jesus said to him, "I do not say to you, up to seven times, but up to seventy-seven times." (NASB)

The seven-day creation week comprises six days and a sabbath day, just like a normal Jewish week. The Torah instructed the Israelites to observe the Year of Jubilee after forty-nine (seven times seven) years had passed, at which time all debts were to be repaid. In Leviticus 25:8 we read, "Count off seven sabbath years—seven times seven years—so that the seven sabbath years amount to a period of forty-nine years." At this time, liberty was to be proclaimed, debts were to be forgiven, people were to return to their own property, and indentured slaves would be freed.

I will look more closely at the sabbath week structure to help better understand the creation week. A key observation is that the creation week is specifically described as lasting seven days, consisting of six days and a sabbath. My view is that the meaning associated with this number would be diminished if the creation week didn't actually consist of six days (of defined length) and a sabbath. I believe that the interpretation of these days as long, vague, and undefined periods of time would result in the word "day" losing its significance. These considerations inform an important part of this book's thesis and lend another reason why I have included the requirement that any acceptable theory about the creation narrative provide a plausible and specific explanation of the Genesis creation days.

In summary, from Genesis to Revelation, from the beginning to the end, cycles of seven are embedded throughout scripture, all of which are associated with the perfect creative and redemptive initiatives of God. We will see how this pattern is important to my week-within-a-week creation model in the chapters to come.

But first, let's begin our discussion of the criteria I will use to determine the credibility of the current theories regarding the origin of our world.

Six

THEORY EVALUATION CRITERIA

MY PROPOSED THEORY on harmonizing the Genesis narrative with a current scientific understanding of the universe and natural history of the Earth must meet certain requirements in order to be considered valid. In the following chapters, I will examine and evaluate existing origin theories to see where they have merit and where they perhaps fall short.

I am here establishing certain criteria by which all theories will be evaluated going forward. My approach is that only a theory which meets every criterion will be considered acceptable. Any theory must:

- Be consistent with scripture and supported by biblical precedents and principles.
- Agree with modern scientific findings.
- Plausibly explain the days of Genesis in terms of defined length.
- Affirm that God is the Creator of all things.
- Show internal consistency and integrity, not contradicting itself in any way.

So any viable and complete theory as defined by the discussion in this book must check all the boxes of the evaluation scorecard below:

EVALUATION SCORECARD

SCRIPTURALLY SUPPORTED	AGREES WITH SCIENCE	PLAUSIBLE 'DAYS' OF DEFINED LENGTH	AFFIRMS GOD IS CREATOR	INTERNAL INTEGRITY

Basically, we are in search of a theory that makes sense of all relevant factors. If a proposed theory about origins isn't supported by the Bible, that theory would be at odds with the testimony of scripture and no alignment would be possible.

However, we must also consider the fact that evolutionary theories about the universe, the Earth, and the development of life are widely held and well-established. My approach, therefore, is not to prove evolution wrong but rather to provide a framework of thought which allows for both science and scripture to be true.

If an evolutionary theory overtly denies God's role as Creator, it cannot provide the complete harmony and explanation which is being sought here. This approach is based on the premise that both the testimony of God's Word and the evidence from natural history should bear witness to the same integrated truth.

As I have previously acknowledged, there is overwhelming scientific evidence for the immensely long age of the universe and our planet. Science also provides geological, paleontological, and anthropological evidence that must be accommodated by any acceptable theory about how everything developed. Any theory that doesn't adequately explain the findings of science would therefore be unacceptable.

The goal of developing a unified theory concerning the creation story is to provide a plausible and acceptable explanation. For this reason, I have included the criterion that any theory must be consistent with the findings of science.

I previously highlighted the significance of the word "day" in the Genesis narrative and elsewhere in the Bible. Accordingly, any thesis which seeks to adequately explain Genesis should provide a plausible, satisfactory answer as to what is meant by the repeated and intentional use of this word in relation to creation. I have therefore also included this requirement as one of the criteria.

As well as aligning with science and scripture, any theory must make sense in and of itself. That is, it cannot contain internal contradictions or falsehoods which would disqualify it. This is the reason for adding this final requirement.

I believe that a theory which satisfies all the suggested criteria would be very valuable and has in fact been earnestly sought for many years. By exploring this subject in the following pages, you can join me in the quest for that elusive theory.

Seven

THEORIES ON RECONCILING GENESIS WITH SCIENCE

> Theory helps us to bear our ignorance of facts.[23]
> —George Santayana

IN THIS CHAPTER, I will review a number of theories that propose to harmonize Genesis and science and evaluate each according to my criteria. This exercise will introduce the evaluation process and give the reader a basic overview of the subject of origins and all its challenges.

Below is a list of the theories which I will very briefly review:

- Gap Theory
- Framework Hypothesis
- Theistic Evolution

GAP THEORY

The gap theory, also known as the Ruin-Restitution Theory, supports the idea of a literal, recent, six twenty-four-hour day creation period. It allows for the vast age of the universe by postulating that the universe, the Earth, and life came into being long before the recent creation events described in scripture. After its creation, the world was destroyed and, after a long gap of time, it was recreated as recorded in Genesis.

Evaluation. The gap theory agrees that the universe is old. But the proposition it advances—that God created the world and then destroyed it and created it again—is not supported by scripture.

While there are several extinction periods evident in the natural history of life on the Earth, no evidence in the fossil record supports the gap predicted by this theory. It therefore appears to have been developed in an attempt to force the Genesis account to accommodate an old universe rather than because of specific biblical or natural evidence.

This theory also proposes that the creation of all things (the second time) was accomplished in six literal twenty-hour days, which is not supported by science.

As a result, this theory does not check all the evaluation criteria.

EVALUATION SCORECARD

✗	✗	✔	✔	✔
SCRIPTURALLY SUPPORTED	AGREES WITH SCIENCE	PLAUSIBLE 'DAYS' OF DEFINED LENGTH	AFFIRMS GOD IS CREATOR	INTERNAL INTEGRITY

FRAMEWORK HYPOTHESIS

The framework hypothesis argues that Genesis 1 is a literary work describing the act of creation. This account is therefore merely a device to convey some rather general ideas about the origin of our world. Its real purpose is not to provide details on the length of time involved or the order of creation. The days are not literal days. Genesis is seen in terms of a philosophical interpretation rather than a literal one, so there is no reason for it to conflict with science.

Evaluation. This theory doesn't meet two of the evaluation criteria. It isn't aligned with the testimony of scripture, nor does it provide any plausible, meaningful explanation for the days of Genesis.

EVALUATION SCORECARD

✗	✓	✗	✓	✓
SCRIPTURALLY SUPPORTED	AGREES WITH SCIENCE	PLAUSIBLE 'DAYS' OF DEFINED LENGTH	AFFIRMS GOD IS CREATOR	INTERNAL INTEGRITY

THEISTIC EVOLUTION

Theistic evolution, also known as God-guided evolution, is the view that God operates through the laws of nature. It suggests that belief in God is compatible with the findings of modern science, including evolution. This theory accepts the scientific consensus on the Big Bang, the age of the universe, the age of the Earth, and the evolution of life.

Many scientists who are also Christians hold some form of this view. They have a sincere faith in Christ but also believe that evolution is a sufficient explanation for the material world. Because the Bible doesn't always align with their scientific understanding, they don't take the Bible as literally as others might. While they don't view the Genesis narrative as being a scientific account, they still believe that man is in need of salvation.

Evaluation. This theory checks the boxes of agreeing with science and ultimately crediting creation to God. But where there are discrepancies between the testimony of scripture and science, theistic evolutionists are required to choose one over the other, and they ultimately choose science.

In that way, this theory discounts the Bible's infallibility. As a result, I don't believe this view supports a faithful interpretation of scripture. Because proponents of this theory don't agree that the

Genesis story can be taken literally, they also don't believe the days of creation have anything more than a symbolic meaning. Therefore, this theory does not fit all my criteria for a complete theory on origins.

EVALUATION SCORECARD

SCRIPTURALLY SUPPORTED	AGREES WITH SCIENCE	PLAUSIBLE 'DAYS' OF DEFINED LENGTH	AFFIRMS GOD IS CREATOR	INTERNAL INTEGRITY
✕	✓	✕	✓	✓

In summary, none of these theories check all the boxes for a unified, consistent theory that harmonizes scripture with science.

In the next few chapters, I will review and evaluate several additional approaches that attempt to harmonize scripture and science. Then I will begin to build the case for my own thesis.

Eight

KABBALIST ORAL TRADITION

> The difficulty lies not so much in developing new
> ideas as in escaping from old ones.[24]
> —John Maynard Keynes

A UNIQUE APPROACH to interpreting and comparing the Earth days to God's creation days is found in Jewish Kabbalist oral tradition. The starting point of this approach is identifying the basic timeline of humanity from Adam onwards. The basis for the Kabbalists' approach is their idea that the time of man since the creation of Adam was to be six thousand years followed by the one thousand years of the millennium rule of Christ on the Earth,[25] as described in Revelation 20:4: *"They came to life and reigned with Christ a thousand years."*

The total of seven thousand years is a week of six one-thousand-year days with a thousand-year millennium sabbath day. This structure mirrors a normal week in Jewish life.

By way of background, the concept of a sabbatical millennial week has been forwarded throughout church history. However, it's not expressly taught in the Bible. Although I make reference to it in this book, and it is of interest, my thesis does not rely upon it.

In his book *The Genesis One Code*, Daniel Friedmann outlines a conversion formula between divine time, creation time, and man's time based on the Kabbalist approach:

> The conversion factor from Divine Time to Human Time is provided for us in Psalms, as interpreted in the Talmud: one Divine Day is 1,000 years of Human Time. Given that a calendar year is 365.25 days, then one divine year, or 365.25 divine days, must equate to 365,250 years of Human Time. Thus to calculate Human Time from Divine Time, we multiply Divine Time by 365,250. Creation Time is converted to Human Time by multiplying it by 7,000 (conversion of Creation Time to Divine Time) and again by 365,250 (conversion of Divine Time to Human Time). One Creation Day is therefore equal to 2.56 billion years of Human Time. The time conversion formula is very simple: 1 Creation Day = 7000 x 1000 x 356.25 = 2.56 billion of our years.[26]

In evaluating this model, I would note that this proposed time conversion has some positive qualities but also several significant drawbacks.

One positive is that it seeks to provide a somewhat rational basis for quantifying the vastly different timescales evident between the creation account and scientific discovery. What is also very important in my view is that Friedmann looks to divide his proposed divine creation days into equal lengths of time.

Its drawbacks, however, are serious. First, if each creation day is 2.56 billion years in length, the creation days do not match up at all with the Earth's geologic and biological history.

For example, in the creation narrative plants were brought forth on day three. If the universe is 13.8 billion years old, plants should have been present nine billion years ago, according to this theory. But science says that this isn't even close to being correct; the Earth is only 4.5 billion years old itself.

And there are other issues. According to this theory, land animals and man (created on day six) should have been in existence starting 2.5 billion years ago. This is not accurate according to modern science.

In summary, while we can perhaps glean insights from the Kabbalist timeline conversion model, we need to take these writings with a grain of salt. This theory does not align with science in terms of the timeline of the universe or the natural history of the Earth.

EVALUATION SCORECARD

✓	✗	✓	✓	✓
SCRIPTURALLY SUPPORTED	AGREES WITH SCIENCE	PLAUSIBLE 'DAYS' OF DEFINED LENGTH	AFFIRMS GOD IS CREATOR	INTERNAL INTEGRITY

For the interested reader, Appendix One reviews another way of explaining how God's time is different from man's time, called time dilation. While not directly related to the thesis of this book, it is an interesting thought exercise.

Nine

YOUNG EARTH CREATION

> The ways of creation are wrapt in mystery. We may
> only marvel, and bow our head.[27] —Albert Einstein

PROPONENTS OF YOUNG Earth creation (YEC) contend that the
six days of creation in Genesis can only be interpreted as actual
twenty-four-hour days. The creation week, therefore, took six reg-
ular human days and occurred approximately six thousand years
ago.

There are several reasons that young Earth creationists are con-
vinced this is the case. One of the main reasons is their belief that
the author of the Genesis account intended to describe actual days
as opposed to long periods of time. In Chapter Four, I referenced
a logistic regression analysis concluding that there is a very high
probability the author intended the creation story to be read as a
historical account.

I also referenced other scriptural evidence in support of the idea
that the days in Genesis are meant to be understood as actual days.
YEC apologists are persuaded that this evidence can only have
meaning within the context of literal twenty-four-hour days.

While I agree with the analysis that the intentional use of the
word "day" is very meaningful and important, I disagree that this

issue can be satisfactorily resolved only by insisting that the days were twenty-four hours long.

In scripture, the word "day" (in Hebrew, *yom*) is sometimes used in ways that clearly do not describe twenty-four-hour periods of time. For example, in Genesis 2:4: *"These are the generations of the heavens and the earth when they were created, in the day that the Lord God made the earth and the heavens"* (ESV). The use of the word "day" here is clearly a reference to a period of time longer than twenty-four hours.

Also, God rested on the seventh day, but there was no closure based on evening and morning mentioned as for the previous six days. This scripture alone suggests that God's view of a day can be much different than ours. Therefore, an inflexible interpretation of the word isn't necessarily warranted.

Young Earth creationists also reference scriptures which they understand to mean that there was no death before Adam sinned. For example, Romans 5:12 says, *"Therefore, just as sin entered the world through one man, and death through sin, and in this way death came to all people, because all sinned…"* They subscribe to the idea that there was no death at all before Adam sinned, not even in animals or plants. Physical death came about only after and as a result of Adam's sin. They point out that before the fall of Adam, God made everything "very good" and conclude that a very good world would not include death.

I contend that such a conclusion isn't in agreement with the vast scientific understanding of the natural history of the Earth. I suggest that the death spoken about by Paul is a spiritual death that infects all of humankind.

It is true, however, that God did say in Genesis 2:17, *"but from the tree of the knowledge of good and evil, you shall not eat, for on the day that you eat from it you will certainly die."*(NASB) This is an interesting verse, as Adam didn't physically die on the twenty-four-hour day during which he sinned. Rather, he continued to live for hundreds of years and didn't die until he was 930 years old.

But if a day can be interpreted as a thousand years, the day on which Adam was told he would die could reference a period of time one thousand years long. The fact that Adam died at the age of 930 perhaps confirms this approach, as God's warning to Adam seems to have transpired and come true: Adam died on the day that he sinned.

These scriptures certainly provide the latitude to interpret the word "day" in Genesis in broader terms, unconstrained by a twenty-four-hour period of time.

That being said, we always need to look at the context in which a word is used. In Genesis, we have a unique situation. The word "day" seems to describe a longer period in some places and a literal day in others. I address this question in Chapter Fourteen, where I establish a biblical definition of the word "day" that is helpful in deciphering the true meaning of the creation story.

Many YEC arguments against a billions-of-years-old universe focus on questioning the reliability of dating technologies used by modern science. However, tools such as radiometric dating and astrophysical tools such as redshifts and spectral analysis are extremely accurate.

For example, physicist Nathan Leefer has shown that the radiometric decay rates of uranium have a possible variation of only two or three parts per 10^{15} over the past thirteen billion years. This means that age measurements of the Earth based on radioactive decay rates are extremely accurate.[28]

An example of such a measurement is from zircon rocks, which contain uranium and have been dated at 4.2 billion years old.[29]

Many other dating processes have been repeated countless times, using a wide variety of tools and conducted by thousands of different scientists. The results obtained have a very low margin of error.

Therefore, any approach to interpreting scripture that involves attacking scientific methodology is untenable. In fact, efforts to refute scientific findings tend to undermine the credibility of YEC proponents and thus serve to discredit the important underlying message of the Bible which they are trying to advance.

In his book *A Matter of Days*, Dr. Hugh Ross records the comments of researchers from the American Association for the Advancement of Science. They write, "Adoption of creationist (i.e., Young Earth Creationist) 'theory' requires, at a minimum, the abandonment of all modern astronomy, much of modern physics and most of the earth sciences."[30]

Adding to this, I would point out that few scientists using both available data and their own research have concluded that the universe and the Earth are both six thousand years old. The only ones presenting such a thesis are YEC scientists, and this is predicated largely on their interpretation of scripture rather than on the merits of all evidence, established facts, or thorough scientific research.

Let's review just two other examples of geologic formations that negate the young Earth creation thesis to demonstrate what I mean.

The first is the white cliffs of Dover in England. These famous cliffs tower 350 feet above the sea. They were formed in the cretaceous period between seventy and one hundred million years ago from fragments of coccoliths, the skeletons of tiny algae. Over many millions of years, these tiny skeletal remains formed white mud on the surface of the seabed. They are so small that a microscope is required in order for one to see them. Billions of skeletal remains would have been deposited over enormous spans of title to form a sedimentary layer that is 350 feet in height. The seabed on which they accumulated was eventually thrust above sea level by tectonic action. It is inconceivable for this geologic feature to have formed in the past six thousand years.[31]

The second example comes from ice cores obtained from glacial deposits. From these samples, evidence of catastrophic geologic events (such as volcanic ash) and climate change from the deep past (such as atmospheric carbon dioxide levels) can be collected and analyzed. Cores from the Antarctic ice sheet preserve up to eight hundred thousand years of the Earth's history.[32] Its layering, created by annual snowfall, helps identify the age of the ice much like tree rings do for trees. This evidence provides conclusive proof that the Earth is very old.

YEC advocates display a strong commitment to scripture, and this is commendable. However, based on the above discussion, I conclude that their thesis does not stand up to scrutiny. In short, it's not supported by the findings of modern science and therefore it does not meet all critical evaluation metrics.

EVALUATION SCORECARD

✓	✗	✓	✓	✓
SCRIPTURALLY SUPPORTED	AGREES WITH SCIENCE	PLAUSIBLE 'DAYS' OF DEFINED LENGTH	AFFIRMS GOD IS CREATOR	INTERNAL INTEGRITY

Ten

DAY-AGE THEORY

> But they deliberately forget that long ago by God's
> word the heavens came into being and the earth
> was formed out of water and by water. (2 Peter 3:5)

NOW I WILL look at another approach to reconciling Genesis with science. The day-age theory seeks to harmonize scripture and science by postulating that the "days" in the creation story are meant to convey long, indefinite periods of time. Day-age advocates accept the findings of science but still attribute creation to God. They are biblical literalists who interpret the meaning of "day" differently.

A prominent proponent of the day-age theory is Canadian astrophysicist Hugh Ross. Ross has written many books and continues to actively highlight the many examples of the finetuning of the universe. I would like to briefly mention a few of the points Ross raised in his book, *A Matter of Days*:

> The two parameters governing the expansion of the
> universe—the mass density and the space-energy
> density—must be fine-tuned. The fine-tuning for the
> space-energy density (dark matter) is more precise
> than 1 part in 10^{120} (that's 120 zeros after the one)

in order to yield a universe of galaxies, stars and planets—that is, a universe suitable for any kind of physical life…

The universe, our galaxy, and solar system exhibit more than 500 different characteristics requiring exquisite fine-tuning for life's existence (any kind of physical life, not just life as we know it)…

The sun is just the right age to provide a stable level of light and heat to allow for advanced life. There is only a short time window of approximately 100,000 years in the life of stars the size of ours where such stability is possible. In the first 50 million years of a sun's existence, its burn rate and temperature are too erratic. Then, for the next 500 million years, X-ray emissions are too intense for life to exist. It is only after 4.6 billion years that the flaring activity of a star such as our Sun would have subsided sufficiently to provide the stability required to support intelligent life.[33]

Theories on how the moon came to orbit the Earth also require an absurd amount of precision, given that the moon's mass compared to the Earth's mass is fifty times greater than the next closest moon-to-host-planet ratio.

In an issue of *Nature*, earth scientist Tim Elliott recently observed, "The sequence of conditions that currently seems necessary in the revised versions of lunar formation have led to philosophical disquiet."[34]

Over and above the difficulties in the formation of the moon is the influence it had in making life on the Earth possible. The moon:

- Created perfect air pressure and just-right heat-trapping capability
- Gave our atmosphere the optimal chemical composition for advanced life
- Allowed mass to gravitationally retain a large (but not too large) quantity of water vapour
- Raised iron in the Earth's core to provide the needed magnetic field to protect life on the Earth from solar X-rays
- Influenced the composition of the Earth's mantle and allowed for plate tectonics
- Provided increased iron content to permit abundant life in the ocean
- Provided long-lasting radioisotopes, which provide heat to create plate tectonics
- Slowed the Earth's rotation to allow advanced life to exist
- Stabilized the Earth's rotational tilt to allow for stable climate variations[35]

This brief summary doesn't do justice to the complexity of all the interactions related just to the moon, which are themselves a tiny fraction of the complexity involved in the formation of the universe. My purpose here is to provide a glimpse into the vast number of complex and interrelated components that are necessary for advanced life to form on our planet.

The day-age theory acknowledges that the measurements and findings of science are correct, but it also maintains that scripture is just as true. This theory has many strengths, particularly as it relates to the appreciation of the required finetuning evident in the universe. Another plus is its recognition of the awesome wonder and beauty of the universe as one of the main reasons to believe in both the God of the Bible and scientific findings.

The day-age theory is closely linked with the concept of the anthropic principle, whereby the sheer complexity of creation seems purposely designed for life. Day-age proponents differ from theistic evolutionists in that they don't believe that unguided evolution by itself is sufficient to explain all that is seen in creation. In this way, the day-age approach can be more easily harmonized with Genesis, allowing its proponents to take the Bible much more literally.

The main reason that the day-age theory is inadequate from my standpoint is that it doesn't address the seemingly intentional use of the word "day" in Genesis. This theory is comfortable with claiming that *yom* can refer to long, undefined periods of time in certain contexts, including the creation account.[36]

But I believe this is not the intended meaning of the word as it's used in this part of Genesis. As noted in Chapter Four, there are strong scriptural reasons to look for a more specific meaning of "day" in this context. By not attaching more importance to the word "day," I believe day-age proponents risk missing something profound.

In summary, the day-age theory meets most of the evaluation criteria of this book. However, it doesn't provide a satisfactory explanation of the word "day" in the biblical creation account. Therefore, it does not meet all criteria. **Score: 4 of 5**

EVALUATION SCORECARD

✓	✓	✗	✓	✓
SCRIPTURALLY SUPPORTED	AGREES WITH SCIENCE	PLAUSIBLE 'DAYS' OF DEFINED LENGTH	AFFIRMS GOD IS CREATOR	INTERNAL INTEGRITY

Eleven

THE BATTLE OF JERICHO MODEL

NOW THAT WE'VE reviewed many theories on how Genesis can be interpreted and found them, based on my criteria, to be somewhat inadequate, I would like to begin to build the case for my new thesis. I will do this over the course of the next few chapters by presenting a number of biblically based models that are useful in establishing important patterns and relevant precedents.

For our first model, I refer to the battle of Jericho. The reader may recall that I mentioned this important biblical event in Chapter Five. By way of reminder, Joshua and the Israelites marched around Jericho once per day for six days and then, on the sabbath, marched around the city seven times before the walls fell.

This format of seven marches on the seventh day reinforces its biblical significance. A visual for this event is shown on the next page.

There are some important narrative features to note here. The first stage of the siege of Jericho consisted of six days. The purpose of God and the Israelites from the start was to enter and capture the city. On the sabbath, their purpose remained the same, but their actions intensified by a factor of seven.

BATTLE OF JERICHO MODEL

7 DAYS

						7 MARCHES
6 MARCHES AROUND JERICHO						
DAY 1	DAY 2	DAY 3	DAY 4	DAY 5	DAY 6	DAY 7

START OF JERICHO SIEGE

START OF SABBATH

ENTERED JERICHO

We see that the sabbath day marches are a subset of the total seven days of the battle of Jericho—a week of marches within a week of marches. I intend to show how this model is valuable in terms of understanding the creation week.

The second biblical model I would like to analyze is Daniel's prophecy of seventy weeks because it reflects some similar patterns and structures.

But before I get to that in the next chapter, I need to first intro-duce a biblical concept that relates to this prophecy and my thesis. It involves identifying God's definition of a prophetic year. This period has also been referred to as an apocalyptic year because one of the places it appears is in the book of Revelation.[38]

As a first step, it may be interesting to learn about how a normal Jewish calendar is established. The Hebrew calendar is lunisolar, which means it is regulated by the positions of both the sun and the moon. It consists of months of twenty-nine or thirty days which begin and end at the time of the new moon. A normal twelve-month year consists of 354 days. However, the solar year is 365.25 days long and exceeds the lunar year by approximately eleven days. As a result, an adjustment needs to be made to match the average days of the Jewish calendar to the solar year.

To accomplish this, an additional month is added to the Jewish year seven times every nineteen years in what is referred to as the Metonic cycle.[39] This additional month is added depending on when the first full moon after the spring equinox arrives. This is called the paschal full moon, paschal coming from the word translated as Passover. The Passover is the Jewish festival celebrating the Exodus from Egypt, further indicating the importance of this event.[40]

To determine the date of important festivals, the start of the Jewish year is the month of Nisan (Rosh Chodashim). If twelve lunar cycles are completed before the spring equinox arrives, the last month is fifty-nine days rather than twenty-nine. So the new year and Passover will normally start at the first full moon after the spring equinox. Through this adjustment, the Jewish calendar aligns itself with the 365-day year of the Gregorian calendar.[41]

The Bible also contains another way of measuring a year. Passages in both the Old and the New Testament speak of a year that's 360 days in length, twelve months of thirty days each. For example, Abraham used a 360-day year that was common in Ur in the land of Chaldees. Sir Isaac Newton stated,

> All nations, before the just length of the solar year was known, reckoned months by the course of the moon, and years by the return of winter, summer, spring and autumn; and in making calendars for their festivals, they reckoned thirty days to a lunar month, and twelve months to a year, taking the nearest round numbers, whence came the division of the ecliptic into 360 degrees.[42]

As mentioned, this 360-day year is found throughout the Bible. For example, Esther 1:4 indicates a year of 360 days in reference to a six-month feast of Xerxes lasting 180 days.

However, most scriptural references to a 360-day year relate to the timing of God's actions or prophetic outcomes. Noah's flood began on the seventeenth day of the second month (Genesis 7:11) and came to an end on the seventeenth day of the seventh month (Genesis 8:4), covering a period of exactly five months. The length of the same period is also given in terms of days, being a *"hundred and fifty days"* (Genesis 7:24, 8:3).

Therefore, the earliest known month used in biblical history was evidently thirty days in length, adding up to a 360-day year.

Also, Daniel 7:25 speaks of a prince who will come and be dominant on the Earth for *"a time, times and half a time"* —in Aramaic, three and a half times. So 360 days multiplied by three and a half times equals 1,260 days.

Revelation 12:6 contains a reference to 1,260 days of persecution of the Jewish saints by a great political ruler. Revelation 12:13–14 refers to this same period of persecution. And Revelation 11:2 says, *"They will trample on the holy city for 42 months."* Therefore, the same period of time is stated three different ways: three and a half years, forty-two months, and 1,260 days. All these timeframes are consistent with a year of 360 days:

3.5 x 360 days = 1,260 days

42 months x 30 days/month = 1,260 days

30 days per month x 12 = 360 days/year

The distinction between the length of a prophetic year of 360 days and our year of 365.25 days may seem trivial, but I believe it is of great importance. If God's creative timeline is to be properly interpreted, we need to understand it from his perspective and how he divides prophetic time. As promised, in the next chapter I will look at one such prophecy.

Twelve

DANIEL'S PROPHECY OF SEVENTY WEEKS

> Seventy "sevens" are decreed for your people
> and your holy city to finish transgression, to put
> an end to sin, to atone for wickedness, to bring in
> everlasting righteousness, to seal up vision and
> prophecy and to anoint the Most Holy Place. (Daniel
> 9:24–27)

I BELIEVE THIS prophecy is one of the most important in the Bible
and has relevance for how the days of creation in Genesis are interpreted. It has fascinated and challenged biblical scholars for centuries, and I believe it provides further validation of some important
principles I seek to establish.

Daniel received this prophecy from the angel Gabriel, who
announces that there will be a period of time (seventy sevens) at the
end of which many transformative events and changes will transpire.
Based on what it says will be accomplished by the end of this prophecy, it clearly refers to the end-times.

For the Jews at the time of Daniel's writing, it was normal "to
render the word 'week' capable of meaning a seven of years almost
as naturally as a seven of days."[43] So the period of seventy sevens
relates to seventy "weeks" of years, or 490 years in total. Recall from

Chapter Five that the number seventy times seven (490) is associated with perfection and completion. In this case, it leads to Christ's perfect redemption of the world.

Starting in Daniel 9:25–26, we read,

> Know and understand this: From the time the word goes out to restore and rebuild Jerusalem until the Anointed One, the ruler, comes, there will be seven "sevens," and sixty-two "sevens." It will be rebuilt with streets and a trench, but in times of trouble. After the sixty-two "sevens," the Anointed One will be put to death and will have nothing.

The declaration to rebuild Jerusalem marks the start of the 490 years. This occurred in the reign of Artaxerxes in 444 BC. The total number of weeks spoken about in these verses of the prophecy is sixty-nine (seven weeks plus sixty-two weeks). It is taken to mean that sixty-nine times seven (483) years will elapse from the time of the announcement to the time when the Messiah (Jesus) will be cut off.

Some analysts have taken the phrase "cut off" to mean "to die." However, author, Wayne Croley convincingly argues that the end of the sixty-nine weeks of this prophecy actually relates to the ascension of Christ rather than his death. This is because Christ was still on the Earth for forty days after his resurrection and was not yet "cut off" from humanity. In his book, *Insights on the End Times*, Croley calculates that Christ's ascension took place on May 12, 33 AD. He then makes the following calculations and explains:

> I converted sixty-nine prophetic weeks into days to begin the search for the start of the first week of Daniel. I did this by turning sixty-nine prophetic

weeks into prophetic years and then prophetic years into days:

One prophetic week = 7 prophetic years
69 weeks of 7 prophetic years = 483 prophetic years
One prophetic year = 360 days
483 prophetic years x 360 days/year = 173,880 days

According to a calendar converter, it was 173,880 days from May 12, 33 AD to April 18, 444 BC.[44]

Based on these calculations, Croley demonstrates that from the time of Artaxerxes's command to rebuild Jerusalem on April 18, 444 BC to Christ's ascension on May 12, 33 AD, there were exactly 173,880 days, in perfect agreement with the prophecy.

The prophecy has not yet been entirely fulfilled and so it continues, with the last "seven" (the seventieth week) still to be completed. We read in Daniel 9:27,

He will confirm a covenant with many for one "seven." In the middle of the "seven" he will put an end to sacrifice and offering. And at the temple he will set up an abomination that causes desolation, until the end that is decreed is poured out on him.

The last week in this cycle is expected to begin when the antichrist arranges an important agreement between Israel and world powers. We know it will involve Israel because Daniel 9:24 states that the prophecy concerns *"your people"* (the Jews) and *"your holy city"* (Jerusalem).

I have illustrated the timeline of Daniel's prophecy of seventy weeks:

DANIEL'S PROPHECY OF 70 WEEKS

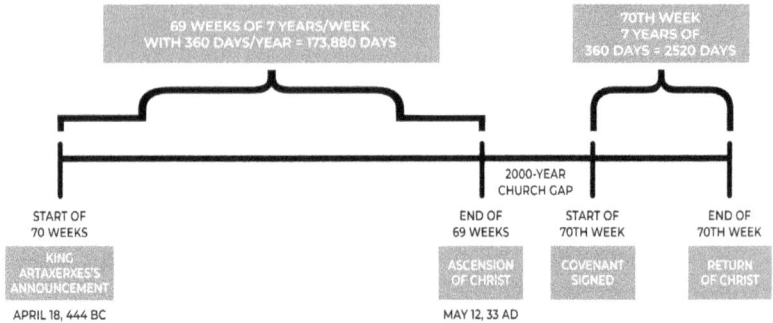

I have also provided a visual representation of this prophecy in the same format used for the battle of Jericho model, which reveals a very similar structure:

DANIEL'S PROPHECY MODEL
70 WEEKS

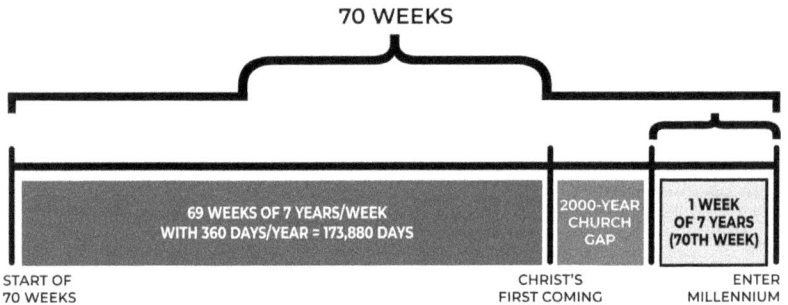

The most common understanding of this prophecy is that a significant gap of time passes between the end of the sixty-ninth week and the start of the seventieth week. Specifically, this gap in time is associated with the church age, or the age of grace, a timespan of approximately two thousand years, up to now.[45]

I would like to analyze how the age gap theory stands up when evaluated against the principles I have identified so far. The seventieth week is clearly related to the first sixty-nine, both of which have the same theme involving future events concerning the Israelites and the holy city. The seventieth week has a clearly defined starting date, with a strong covenant being confirmed or ratified. The termination of the seventieth week is also clearly defined, as Daniel 9:24 proclaims:

> Seventy "sevens" are decreed for your people and your holy city to finish transgression, to put an end to sin, to atone for wickedness, to bring in everlasting righteousness, to seal up vision and prophecy and to anoint the Most Holy Place.

Based on this passage, I believe the prophecy relates to the completion of the entire age of Adam's race on the Earth prior to Christ's return. The end date for this prophecy will therefore be the end of the current age. If this is true, this last "seven" has not yet been completed.

When the seventieth week is viewed as its own mini-cycle within the greater cycle of seventy weeks, it is clear that it must also terminate at the same time. Therefore, we can reach a perfectly logical conclusion about the gap between the sixty-ninth and seventieth week.

Let me elaborate.

The prophecy starts on April 18, 444 BC. If the seventy "weeks" had occurred consecutively, the entire seventy-year program would have terminated at the year 40 AD. But the events associated with the end of the seventieth week have not yet occurred. This means there must be a gap.

As the seventieth week appears to be associated with the winding-up of all earthly things, it is therefore reasonable to conclude that the last week of this prophecy relates to the seven-year tribulation period. The tribulation occurs at the end-times and is spoken about in Revelation and many other places in the Bible.

For example, in Matthew 24:21 Christ warns us about this period: *"For then there will be great distress, unequaled from the beginning of the world until now—and never to be equaled again."*

In Daniel, this seven-year period starts with the confirmation of a covenant, which is then broken in the middle of the "week." Concerning the period of time that passes after the covenant is broken, Revelation refers to it as lasting three and a half years, forty-two months, or 1,260 days, all of which are based on God's prophetic year of 360 days.

The prophet Jeremiah apocalyptically refers to this period of tribulation as the *"time of trouble for Jacob"* (Jeremiah 30:7), Jacob being a synecdoche or representative for the entire nation of Israel.

Currently, the tribulation has not yet started, so it's safe to say that this portion of the prophecy has not yet been completed. Based on this analysis, I consider the gap theory to be valid. I therefore expect that this prophecy will continue to have great meaning for mankind in the future.

In addition, the patterns associated with this prophecy will greatly benefit the analysis of Genesis.

Daniel's prophecy is all about the redemptive plan that God has decreed or ordained for Israel, and it is related to many other prophecies concerning the covenants God made with Abraham, Moses, and David to establish Israel in the land forever and, ultimately, to eternally restore Israel.

Based on our review of this prophecy, a number of patterns and takeaways are apparent:

- There is a predominant use of the number seven.
- The seventy times seven format in this prophecy is associated with God's perfection, supporting the idea that the prophecy's culmination leads to perfection on the Earth (such as the millennium).

- It is an example of the prophetic year of God lasting 360 days rather than 365.25 days (a human year).
- It demonstrates the exactness of God's predictions and timing involving historical events.
- A portion of time in this prophecy has not yet started or been completed.
- A smaller section, the seventieth week, is a subset of the total program of seventy weeks. Both parts of the prophecy have the same termination date: the return of Christ.
- Both the longer and shorter parts of the prophecy have the same theme: the redemption plan of God.

In summary, this model creates a structure that is very similar to that of the battle of Jericho. In particular, the last week of the prophecy is a subset of the total prophetic timeline—that is, it is a week within the seventy weeks.

In the next chapter, I will review another biblical model with similar characteristics.

Thirteen

THE WILDERNESS MODEL

> A voice of one calling: "In the wilderness prepare
> the way for the Lord; make straight in the desert a
> highway for our God." (Isaiah 40:3)

ONE MIGHT WONDER what the wilderness has to do with the creation narrative. The Bible is filled with repeated patterns, and important clues can be found by studying them, helping us to discover new truths and validate ideas about the creation story.

The wilderness cycle is one of those patterns.

Before I begin my analysis, it's worth reflecting on what it means in the Bible to be in the wilderness. It means to be lost, even abandoned, perhaps to be in doubt or confused and in mental anguish. Oftentimes it's associated with God's judgment or the consequences of sin. It's also related to being far from home, in distress and under physical hardship. In the wilderness, hope ebbs and one feels a deep longing for peace in a new home and the promise of better things to be fulfilled. It's a time when God prepares his people's hearts for his purposes.

In this context, we can appreciate the consequences of the acute polarization between science and faith in the world. Some who have had trouble reconciling the claims of the Bible and the findings of science have abandoned their faith and made others feel that religious belief isn't even worthy of consideration. No one is comfortable holding a position or trying to defend a belief if they lack logical or convincing arguments. If a person can't properly defend the tenets of their faith, they might stop embracing these beliefs due to a desire to maintain their sense of personal integrity.

Young students entering university sometimes feel a need to keep their faith hidden or abandon it entirely so they won't be the target of intellectual ridicule. People are thus pushed deep into a theological wilderness where there seems to be no way out.

With these thoughts in mind, I believe it's time to step forward in our studies, out of the wilderness, and wade in the waters as the children of Israel did. I will provide four examples of wilderness experiences found in scripture.

The first is Noah's flood, when God's judgment of the world led to death and hardship. Noah's family needed to depend on God to prepare themselves for a new future. After the flood they found themselves far from home, typical of wilderness experiences.

It's notable that it rained for forty days and forty nights. We will see that the number forty, and multiples thereof, are associated with all the wilderness events I will review.

For our second example, we come to Jesus's temptation in the desert. He was alone and without food, suffering hardships and testing of body and mind as he prepared to usher mankind into a new Promised Land and establish the kingdom of God.

Before he left the desert, completely depleted of physical strength, he faced a final test. Satan approached and tested him with three offers to renounce God and worship him. Christ didn't flinch. He rebuked Satan, then departed from the wilderness and its forty days of testing and preparation.

The third example relates to Israel's wilderness experience of four hundred years of captivity in Egypt. The Lord had said to Abraham,

"Know for certain that for four hundred years your descendants will be strangers in a country not their own and that they will be enslaved and mistreated there" (Genesis 15:13). This wilderness experience was a long and cruel period of captivity.

The Bible recounts that after their oppression in Egypt, the Israelites escaped Pharoah and crossed through the Red Sea. They found themselves in the desert wilderness of Sinai, where they wandered for forty years while being tested by God.

This time of testing and struggling in the desert of Sinai is our fourth example of a wilderness experience.

As I prepare to analyze and compare these biblical events, a moment should be taken to reflect on the importance of the Exodus event. The Exodus marked a new beginning for the Israelites as a special nation, purposefully and miraculously chosen by God to be his people. Leviticus 11:45 says, *"I am the Lord, who brought you up out of Egypt to be your God; therefore be holy, because I am holy."*

The Exodus is referenced in the Bible 149 times, including mentions of the feasts which were established as its memorials: Passover, the Feast of Weeks, and the Feast of Tabernacles. This biblical emphasis reflects the importance of the Exodus in the life of the nation.

The Torah's commandment (mitzvah) exhorts faithful Jews to eat matzah, a cracker-like unleavened bread, every day: "in order that you will remember the day of the Exodus from the land of Egypt all the days of your life."[46]

Rabbi Irving Greenberg wrote,

> When Jews observe Passover, they are commemorating what is arguably the most important event of all time—the Exodus from Egypt. If for no other reason than the fact that the Exodus directly or

indirectly generated many of the important events cited by other groups, this is the event of human history.[47]

The Exodus event was filled with direct miracles and signs, the abundance of which demonstrate the importance of this new nation to God. One could argue that this was the most significant display of God's creative power and purposes on the Earth since its creation. Deuteronomy 4:34 confirms this:

> Has any god ever tried to take for himself one nation out of another nation, by testings, by signs and wonders, by war, by a mighty hand and an outstretched arm, or by great and awesome deeds, like all the things the Lord your God did for you in Egypt before your very eyes?

In summary, and in light of the importance of the Exodus, any biblical patterns and principles related to this event should be considered meaningful and worthy of serious reflection.

Below is an illustration of the timeline of Israel's wilderness experiences in Egypt and Sinai:

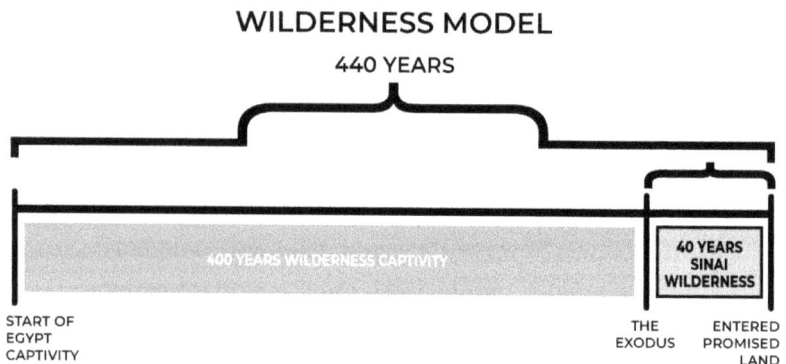

WILDERNESS MODEL
440 YEARS

400 YEARS WILDERNESS CAPTIVITY

40 YEARS SINAI WILDERNESS

START OF EGYPT CAPTIVITY

THE EXODUS

ENTERED PROMISED LAND

The total length of time of this wilderness experience was 440 years. This period ended when the children of Israel entered the Promised Land. The Sinai wilderness experience was a small subset of the total time involved and ended when the Israelites entered the Promised Land.

Let's now look at the structural similarities of the wilderness accounts:

- Israel's first wilderness event (four hundred years) led immediately to the second wilderness event (forty years).
- The wilderness events are associated with timeframes in multiples of forty: four hundred years, forty years, and forty days.
- The Sinai experience was a subset of the larger Exodus experience.
- Both the Exodus and Sinai wilderness events had the same termination point: their arrival in the Promised Land.

We can see the patterns to be found in these scriptural wilderness accounts. A pattern involving multiples of the number forty ties the events together.

The wilderness model looks very much like the previous models we have reviewed so far, specifically in the way the last section serves as a subset of the total.

Before moving on, I would like to expand on the wilderness model a bit further in relationship to the concept of the millennial sabbatical week. As we touched on in Chapter Eight, some theologians maintain that the millennial sabbatical week is a week of thousand-year days constituting humanity's existence, commencing with Adam and culminating with a sabbath that occurs during Christ's reign of one thousand years. I offer this information for the reader's consideration, bearing in mind that this model is inferred from Scripture and not expressly taught. That said, the millennial week was incorporated into the beliefs of some of the early church fathers, as can be seen in the following writings.

Around 100 AD, Barnabas wrote:

> Attend, my children, to the meaning of this expression, "He finished in six days." This implieth that the Lord will finish all things in six thousand years, for a day is with Him a thousand years.[48]

And later, Irenaeus wrote,

> For the day of the Lord is as a thousand years; and in six days created things were completed: it is evident, therefore, that they will come to an end at the sixth thousandth year.[49]

Based on this interpretation, the millennial reign of Christ, lasting one thousand years, is associated with a sabbath rest. The preceding week would consist of six days of equal length—that is, six times one thousand, or six thousand years. See below for an illustration of the millennial week:

MILLENNIAL WEEK PROPHECY MODEL

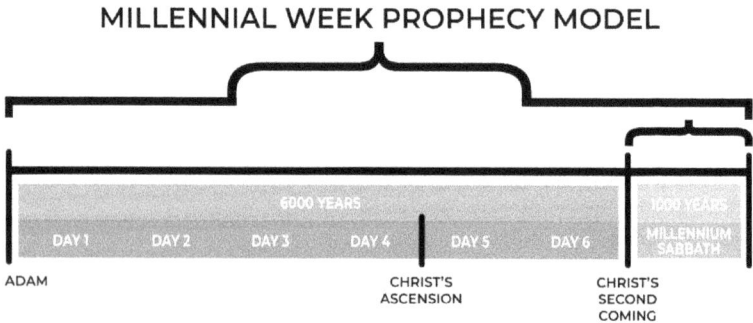

| 6000 YEARS | | | | | | 1000 YEARS |
| DAY 1 | DAY 2 | DAY 3 | DAY 4 | DAY 5 | DAY 6 | MILLENNIUM SABBATH |

ADAM

CHRIST'S ASCENSION

CHRIST'S SECOND COMING

This model exhibits a similar structure to the others I have reviewed thus far. Specifically, the millennium is a subset of the whole seven-thousand-year program. The entire week shares the same theme: mankind's term on Earth. The seven-thousand-year timeframe ends at the same time as the thousand-year millennium.

A supporting argument for the validity of the millennial week comes from the genealogy of Adam up to Christ. Based on a calculation of ages from the Masoretic Text version of the Old Testament, Adam was created in 4004 BC and cast out of the garden at some time after that.[50] Thus, six thousand years have now passed since that event, and two thousand years since the crucifixion of Christ. Mankind, according to this model, is currently situated right before the end-times prophesied in the Bible and the millennial reign of Christ.

Although the millennial week cycle has the same structure of six-days-and-a-sabbath, its timescale is different than a typical week's. Like the wilderness events, vastly different timeframes are at work for similar-themed cycles. Specifically, seven thousand years for the millennial week of mankind versus seven days for a human week, versus seven years in a week of years, versus seven days of some presumed length for God's creation week, including the sabbath.

THE GREATER WILDERNESS MODEL

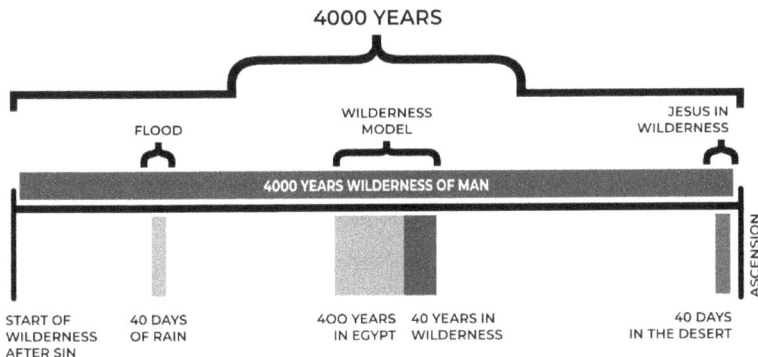

In the course of my studies I have identified an additional wilderness structure which I will call the greater wilderness model (shown above). The premise for this model is that mankind's wilderness experience began when Adam and Eve sinned. Within the millennial week, the greater wilderness period would have begun at the moment of Adam and Eve's expulsion from the garden and would have ended at the ascension of Christ. This endpoint is chosen because this is when Christ opened the door back to God. His ascension marked the beginning of the age of grace, or the church age.

There are several important patterns in this timeline. The most crucial is that the total wilderness experience lasted four thousand years. This is in line with the millennial week calendar of seven thousand years being separated into three timeframes: four thousand years from creation to Christ, two thousand years from Christ to the millennium, and one thousand years for the millennium. Within these four thousand years, four other wilderness events are associated with the number forty, as shown in the illustration (and in the previously discussed models). All four of them therefore represent small subsets of the greater wilderness model.

The forty days Jesus spent in the wilderness, shown near the endpoint of this model, create a pattern similar to the other models we have already looked at.

Below I illustrate this specific relationship in the same format as the other models. Jesus's time on the Earth leads mankind out of the greater wilderness. The original wilderness model is shown alongside it for comparison purposes.

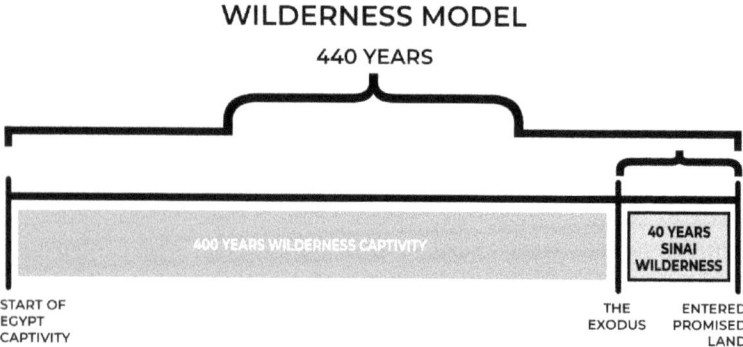

WILDERNESS MODEL
440 YEARS

400 YEARS WILDERNESS CAPTIVITY

40 YEARS
SINAI
WILDERNESS

START OF
EGYPT
CAPTIVITY

THE
EXODUS

ENTERED
PROMISED
LAND

THE GREATER WILDERNESS MODEL

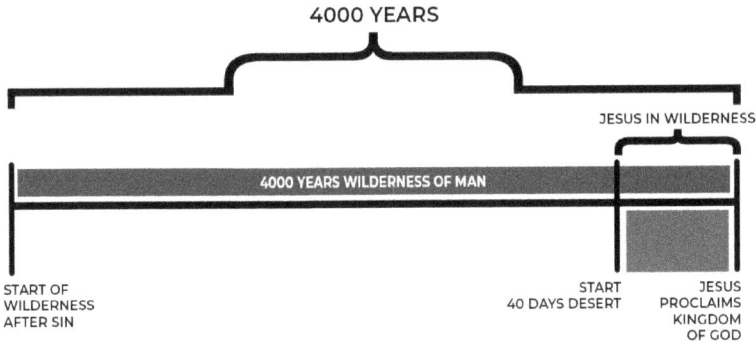

4000 YEARS

JESUS IN WILDERNESS

4000 YEARS WILDERNESS OF MAN

START OF
WILDERNESS
AFTER SIN

START
40 DAYS DESERT

JESUS
PROCLAIMS
KINGDOM
OF GOD

I consider this model to represent a very profound theological concept: Christ entering the wilderness on mankind's behalf. Once he left the desert and began his ministry, Jesus proclaimed the coming of the kingdom of God. For example, Luke 8:1 records, *"After this, Jesus traveled about from one town and village to another, proclaiming the good news of the kingdom of God."* Jesus's subsequent redemptive work allowed for the restoration of man's relationship with God. That relationship had been lost due to the sin of Adam, which then led to the wilderness experience of mankind. So what was lost by Adam was restored by Christ.

In addition, this illustration reflects the pattern of a wilderness within a wilderness that leads to a new Promised Land. The end of the wilderness brought man to the doorway of the kingdom of God.

In the preceding chapters, I have established a number of biblical models which provide part of the basis for my thesis. In the next chapter, I want to return to the importance of how we interpret the word "day" before we put it all together.

Fourteen

THE DEFINITION OF A DAY

> A thousand years in your sight are like a day that has just gone by, or like a watch in the night. (Psalm 90:4)

UP TO THIS point, I have established a number of principles that I want to recap briefly before we move on to our discussion of the definition of a "day" in the creation story:

- Weekly cycles have a definite start time.
- Weekly cycles have a definite completion time.
- The six-day-and-sabbath week is a fundamental biblical cycle.
- Biblical cycles can exist in time multiples of each other.
- There can be a descending order of times between such cycles—four hundred years, forty years, seventy weeks, one week, etc.
- Cycles of related events can be subsets of each other (such as wilderness cycles).

Based on these patterns and principles, we can construct a new, useful, biblically supported definition of the word "day." We need to recognize that the most important and widely used cycle of God is the weekly cycle. Specifically, the six-day-and-sabbath cycle for a total of seven days. We also need to remember that the words "week," "day," and "year" can be used interchangeably in scripture depending on the context and/or time period involved (Leviticus 25:8, Daniel 9:24). And if you recall, in our discussion of the day-age theory we learned that the Hebrew word for day is *yom*, which in certain contexts can refer to an extended period of time.

In the creation cycle, God works six days of the week and then rests on the sabbath. In the Jewish sabbath week, man works six days and then rests. Likewise, in Leviticus 25:4 the Israelites were commanded, *"But in the seventh year the land is to have a year of sabbath rest, a sabbath to the Lord."* This structure represents a week of years, with the seventh year being a sabbath. Based on this, I suggest that the meaning of the word "day" is characterized by a function of activity as well as by a set time.

Also, the use of the word "week" is used in many different time-frames. Therefore, the time for a "day" can also be used in multiple timeframes. For example, the length of a day in a normal human workweek is different from the length of a day in a week of years or, theoretically, a millennial week. I believe that recognizing this variability is critically important.

Also significant, if somewhat obvious, is the fact that days are individual parts of a week.

Based on all this, I offer the following definition of a biblical day: one of six equal periods of time plus a sabbath within a weekly time-frame, each defined by a start and end and often related to a scope of work being completed. Weeks can encompass different time-frames depending on the context. Therefore, the length of a particular day will be in proportion to the timescale of the associated week.

This new, biblically derived definition of the word "day" is consistent with the use of the word in scripture and has profound implications for my analysis of Genesis.

The reference to work in our definition is important. The creation week is when God completed all his work. It is clear that God has used his scriptures to establish a strong connection between six days and work. Therefore, it must be significant. For the purposes of analyzing and understanding the creation story, this connection warrants inclusion in the definition of the word "day."

In Rabbinic Jewish law, day and night are taken to be twelve hours long, for ceremonial purposes. For example, noon is always the sixth hour. And the day runs from nightfall to nightfall.[51] After the evening and the night comes the morning, when the work of the day can begin.

This is also the pattern of the Genesis narrative. The use of the phrase *"and there was evening, and there was morning"* (Genesis 1:5, 8, 13, 19, 23, 31) reflects the pattern of work life, with the scope of work done on each day being separated by night. This pattern is used to help readers relate their weekly work lives to God's creation workweek. It provides a parallel between a twenty-four-hour day for man and God's creation day.

I believe, this evening/morning phrase has become a huge stumbling block to a proper interpretation of the narrative, because it has traditionally been interpreted to mean that the creation days were twenty-four hours long.

But how else could there be evening and morning? This is a reasonable question.

I believe that this intentional phrasing accomplishes two things.

First, rather than prove that days were twenty-four hours in length, it confirms that the creation days were of specific and equal length as opposed to long, vague periods of time.

Secondly, it serves to highlight and bookmark the scope of work completed by God on each creation day. These creative acts were separated by time like night separates the workdays of man, perhaps allowing nature to take its course over millions or billions of years before a new command was issued by God.

One could ask, how else could God have effectively and efficiently communicated all these concepts to readers except through the use of this phrase, that there was evening and there was morning?

In Chapter Four, I referred to the many examples in the Bible where a number is used in relation to the word "day." For example, we read in Acts 20:6, *"But we sailed from Philippi after the Festival of Unleavened Bread, and five days later joined the others at Troas, where we stayed seven days."* Some see this use of numbered days as a pattern with a specific meaning—that whenever numbers are used in relation to days, twenty-four-hour days are involved. This is the argument used by advocates for a young Earth: because the days of Genesis are numbered, they must be twenty-four-hour timeframes.

I do not believe this to be true.

It is true that almost all references to the word "day" in the Bible relate to twenty-four hours in the affairs of man. But this precedent doesn't always apply to God's initiatives. For example, in Hosea 6:1–2 we read,

> Come, let us return to the Lord. He has torn us to pieces but he will heal us; he has injured us but he will bind up our wounds. After two days he will revive us; on the third day he will restore us, that we may live in his presence.

Without going into a great deal of eschatological detail, let me just say that I believe this passage symbolically relates to Israel returning to the Lord at the time of the tribulation. The idea of being revived after two days, and raised up on the third, clearly does not only relate to Christ rising on the third day; it also relates to the two thousand years after Christ when Israel will be regathered as a nation and to the thousand-year reign of Christ, adding up to a total of three thousand years.[52]

In addition, we are told in Genesis 2:2, *"By the seventh day God had finished the work he had been doing; so on the seventh day he rested from all his work."* The seventh day didn't have an evening or a morning and is thus an ongoing period of time, meaning that it was not a twenty-four-hour period.

Based on these precedents, with numbered days able to represent days of longer periods of time, we can comfortably ascribe longer periods of time to the days of creation.

Getting back to the definition of a "day," let's consider a typical human workday. It doesn't always involve doing one job, but rather includes many activities and goals to be accomplished.

For example, imagine that you are embarking on a Friday of work at your cabin. It might involve doing yard work in the morning, starting the foundations of a new deck in the afternoon, and then getting an old picnic table painted before supper. This defines the scope of work you may accomplish.

Imagine now that at some point during the following week, you casually mention to a friend that you finally got around to painting your picnic table last Friday. In doing so, you wouldn't necessarily tell them that you had actually purchased the paint and sanded down the picnic table on Thursday in preparation for painting on Friday. And you also might not tell them that as a child you helped your grandfather build that picnic table at his cabin and had been keeping it for years until the time came when you owned a cabin of your own.

At the risk of belabouring the point, I am trying to identify the following principles:

- The word "day," in the context of work, is defined by the related scope of work or development occurring during the timespan of that day.

- The work of one "day" often involves the effort of preparing for the work of the next day.
- The length of a "day" depends on the timeframes involved. For example, a day in a human workweek is twenty-four hours long, but a day a week of years is one year. And in the context of a millennial week, a day would be one thousand years long.
- Long periods in time of equal length can be understood as "days."

In summary, arriving at a correct definition of the word "day" is indispensable in understanding the Genesis narrative. The definition offered here will help demonstrate the nature of the creation days and weeks, demonstrating how this creation account can be reconciled with the findings of science regarding the age of the Earth and our universe.

Fifteen

WHEN DOES THE CREATION WEEK BEGIN?

> The beginning is the most important part of the
> work.[53] — Plato

A FOUNDATIONAL QUESTION in our quest for a unified origins theory is this: when does creation week begin? The answer is critical to properly understanding the timing of the Genesis narrative. Based on Genesis 1:1, the creation week begins *"in the beginning."* If we assume that this is consistent with the best current scientific measurements regarding the age of the universe, the starting point was about 13.8 billion years ago.

The approach that assumes the creation week started *"in the beginning"* has most commonly been used by theologians and creationists throughout history, although the timeframes associated with their views might have differed. That is, God created the universe and the world in six days, however long those days might be.

But the thesis of this book is that a more detailed interpretation is needed.

In Genesis 1:2 we read, *"Now the earth was formless and empty, darkness was over the surface of the deep, and the Spirit of God was hovering over the waters."* I believe that when God was hovering over the waters, the Earth already existed in a primordial state, having been created at some unknown time in the past. That the Earth was already covered with water is also significant. If it was already formed, in orbit around the sun, and had water on its surface, a very long time must have already passed based on data about normal geologic and astronomical processes.

Unless a supernatural cause is ascribed to an event or process, it is assumed in this book that normal laws of physics are at work. For example, in Genesis 1 the phrases *"God said"* and *"God made"* overtly imply God's intervention. That is not to say that God only does miraculous things if they are announced. He is not limited to what is recorded in scripture and has certainly intervened supernaturally many times in human history. But he also allows the normal laws of physics—such as gravity, electromagnetism, chemical and biological processes, and mathematical relationships—to affect the physical dimension.

Jeremiah 33:25–26 states,

> This is what the Lord says: "If I have not made my covenant with day and night and established the laws of heaven and earth, then I will reject the descendants of Jacob and David my servant and will not choose one of his sons to rule over the descendants of Abraham, Isaac and Jacob."

From this, we understand that long ago God firmly established the laws of the universe. So we can affirm that he intentionally created the heavens and the Earth, but also that it took billions of years and largely involved natural processes.

To demonstrate what I mean by this, let's compare the creation of the universe to God's creation of the nation of Israel. We can trace its start from Abraham and continue through Jacob, Moses, and the Exodus, and then throughout its history and turmoil to the time when

Israel was established in the land with the law, a priesthood, and a temple. This took a very long time.

Certainly, this miraculous journey was directed by God and played out for his purposes, but it was a long process nonetheless. Most of the events and activities of the Israelites were driven by normal physical laws and circumstances. But some events and experiences—manna from heaven or the parting of the Red Sea, for example—were miraculous interventions by God.

For illustration purposes, let's imagine that God was describing the process of creating the nation of Israel and wrote an alternate version of Genesis 1:1: "In the beginning, I created Abraham and all his descendants, who would become my people Israel." Then, in Genesis 1:2, he might have gone on to communicate the period of the Exodus: "Now Israel was in bondage in Egypt and I heard the cries of my people." You could appreciate the vast difference in time and circumstances between these two verses, with many missing details. But that wouldn't mean they were inaccurate or unimportant. The creation narrative can be seen to follow this same pattern.

Using this analogy, let's look again at Genesis 1:2, in which God's creative activity appears to commence at a time when the Earth was already in a watery state. This doesn't seem to align with a starting point from nothing, which we often assume it should because of the phrase *"in the beginning."*

According to science, the Earth was formed some nine billion years after the universe began. In addition, it would take a long time for natural processes to convert the planet from a primordial molten core to one with a surface covered in land and water. Science confirms this to be true.

To develop this idea a bit more, in Job 38:1–9 we get valuable insight into the work and processes of creation. I believe this passage concludes at the exact time that Genesis 1:2 begins. God is recounting and elaborating on the time when he was *"hovering over the waters"* and the Earth was covered in darkness:

> Then the Lord spoke to Job out of the storm. He said: "Who is this that obscures my plans with words without knowledge? Brace yourself like a man; I will question you, and you shall answer me.
>
> "Where were you when I laid the earth's foundation? Tell me, if you understand. Who marked off its dimensions? Surely you know! Who stretched a measuring line across it? On what were its footings set, or who laid its cornerstone—while the morning stars sang together and all the angels shouted for joy?
>
> "Who shut up the sea behind doors when it burst forth from the womb, when I made the clouds its garment and wrapped it in thick darkness..." (Job 38:1–9)

I would argue that *"in the beginning"* refers back to the time that astronomers call the Big Bang and continues up until the moment when *"the Spirit of God was hovering over the waters"* (Genesis 1:2). Billions of years elapse between these two moments.

This reading does raise some natural questions. In Genesis 2:1–2 we are told, *"Thus the heavens and the earth were completed in all their vast array. By the seventh day God had finished the work he had been doing; so on the seventh day he rested from all his work."* This indicates that the scope of work in the six days of creation includes making the heavens and the Earth.

If the start of creation is pegged at the beginning of the universe, and if each day was of equal length, then the full 13.8 billion years would have to be divided by six. This would mean that each day was 2.3 billion years in length, leaving us with the same problem as the

Kabbalist theory: if plants were formed on day three, day three would have had to occur nine billion years ago. Since the Earth is only 4.5 billion years old, this approach clearly doesn't work.

On the other hand, if creation started when God hovered over the water, keeping in mind that the Earth is only 4.5 billion years old, we have another intractable problem: science confirms that the universe is almost three times that age. If the age of the Earth is used as our starting point for calculating the length of the days of creation, each day would be 750 million years (4.5 billion divided by six). Days of this length wouldn't match the Earth's natural history and the appearance of life any better than 2.3 billion years would.

For example, fish were created on day five, between 1.5 billion and 750 million years ago according to the new starting point. In sharp contrast, the fossil records show that an abundance of aquatic life appeared during the Cambrian explosion, five hundred million years ago.

And then we come back to plants on day three. Based on the above division of days, the third day would have begun three billion years ago. This still doesn't agree with the scientific data concerning the fossil record of plants.

My conclusion regarding these inconsistencies is that neither of these scenarios passes the evaluation criteria set forward in this book, since they don't provide a plausible length of the creation days or match the science.

The purpose of this discussion is to highlight the challenges involved in reconciling the scientific record with the story of creation in scripture. I believe that my theory regarding the length of each creation day will show how these significant challenges can be overcome both from a biblical and scientific standpoint.

Sixteen

LET THERE BE LIGHT

> The true light that gives light to everyone was
> coming into the world. He was in the world, and
> though the world was made through him, the world
> did not recognize him. (John 1:9–10)

LET'S NOW ANALYZE the creation narrative more closely, keeping in mind that any theory purporting to harmonize Genesis with science must meet all the criteria set out in Chapter Six. It must:

- Be supported by scripture.
- Agree with science.
- Provide a plausible explanation of days.
- Affirm that God is the Creator of all things.
- Have internal consistency/integrity.

Once the new method of interpretation for the creation story has been presented in full, I will test it in the same way as the others to see how well it stands up.

Let's begin our study with a close inspection of Genesis 1:3. When God spoke the majestic and eternal words *"Let there be light,"* what was his frame of reference? The verse prior tells us that he was hovering above the waters of the Earth with darkness all around. I believe that this thick darkness was due to an atmosphere opaque from constant volcanic activity and chemical processes, so heavy and thick that the light of the sun couldn't penetrate it. It wasn't just that the sun itself couldn't be seen behind a thick canopy of gasses, debris, and cloud cover; the surface of the Earth was virtually pitch black all the time.

So what was God's frame of reference? He was positioned either directly above the Earth or near the surface of the planet's deep waters.

Before continuing, I should note that the idea of the sun being hidden by a dark atmosphere at the point in time referenced by Genesis 1:2 is not new, nor is it my own. But I feel it is worth mentioning because it markedly differs from young Earth creation theory, which maintains that the sun was actually created on day four.

Although the Genesis narrative states the sun was made on the fourth day, the verb used in that verse is *haya*, which means "to exist, happen or come to pass." This contrasts with the verbs *bara*, *asa*, and *yasar*, which are used in relation to God's creation of life and which mean "to make, fashion or form."[54]

The use of this verb supports the interpretation I have presented of Genesis 1:14. In addition, the proposition that the sun already existed but its light merely became visible on day four is consistent with basic principles of astronomy and physics. The sun being created after the Earth and light itself is not.

Continuing our discussion of God's frame of reference, we can ask when the six-day-and-sabbath creation week began. I believe it began when God issued His command, *"Let there be light"* (Genesis 1:3). We can be certain of this because the first day ended after light appeared and God's work was successfully completed.

And when did the six creation days come to an end? They ended after the creation of Adam and Eve. Genesis 1:31 states, *"God saw all that he had made, and it was very good. And there was evening, and there was morning—the sixth day."*

After this, God rested on the seventh day.

This creation week follows the six-days-and-sabbath pattern discussed so often in the rest of this book. It would be more accurate to say that the creation week established the pattern for all biblical six-days-and-sabbath cycles that were to follow.

Now we can ask, how long were the days in this creation cycle? Based on the structure of all six-days-and-sabbath weeks and the newly established definition of "day," we can conclude that each day would be one-sixth the length of the total creation time.

Let's now take a look at Genesis 2:1–3:

> Thus the heavens and the earth were completed in all their vast array. By the seventh day God had finished the work he had been doing; so on the seventh day he rested from all his work. Then God blessed the seventh day and made it holy, because on it he rested from all the work of creating that he had done.

This account of God's creation week includes the creation of the heavens and the Earth and everything else.

Let's ask some questions about this creation week.

When did the creation week of Genesis 2 begin? The answer is found in Genesis 2:1. It began at the beginning of the universe, because the heavens are included in what had been completed in the scope of the week's work.

When did this week end? It ended after the creation of all things, including Adam and Eve, according to Genesis 2:2.

What is the length of a day in this creation week? The answer is the same as before—one-sixth of the total creation time.

But here is where we come to a critical point. We have two week-ly cycles, each of which appears to begin at a different time. The first week started while God was hovering over the Earth, and the second week started when the universe began. These weeks must have different lengths, and the length of the associated days within those weeks must therefore also be different.

This is my epiphany: we are actually reading about two different weeks. I believe that this insight is profound and has transforma-tive ramifications for the way we will read scripture going forward. It introduces a unique and meaningful perspective to the narrative which will be shown to have significant implications.

THE WEEK-WITHIN-A-WEEK CREATION MODEL

My thesis is that the correct way to understand the timeline of cre-ation is to recognize that God reveals two different creation weeks in Genesis. The first is the creation week described in Genesis 2, which commenced at the beginning of time. We will call this the Universe Cre-ation Week. It started approximately 13.8 billion years ago, based on the most recent scientific consensus regarding the age of the universe.

The second creation week is described in Genesis 1:2. It com-menced at some point in time after the Earth had already been in exis-tence for billions of years. We will call this the Earth Creation Week. I believe this week started approximately two billion years ago.

In addition, the Universe Creation Week overlaps with the Earth Creation Week.

I propose that the length of a day in the Earth Creation Week be calculated as one-sixth of the time between the moment when God said *"Let there be light"* while hovering over the Earth and the moment when Adam and Eve were created.

I propose that the length of a day in the Universe Creation Week be calculated as one-sixth of the time between the beginning of the universe and the creation of Adam and Eve. This means that:

- The length of each day in the Earth Creation Week is the same as the others in that week.
- The length of each day in the Universe Creation Week is the same as the others in that week.
- The length of a day in the Earth Creation Week is very different from the length of a day in the Universe Creation Week.

Let's state this another way. The period of time from the Big Bang to the creation of Adam can be divided into six days and started 13.8 billion years ago. The period of time from God hovering over the primordial Earth to the creation of Adam can also be divided into six days, but this week covered much less time.

The creation story in Genesis therefore must reference two different yet related six-day sequences.

We think of the Earth Creation Week as a small six-day subset of the larger six-day Universe Creation Week, or a week within a week. We have seen this pattern many times before.

The below chart depicts the relationship between the Universe Creation Week (UCW) and the Earth Creation Week (ECW). I illustrate how the UCW days are of equal length, with the sixth day being composed of the six smaller but also equal-length days of the ECW:

UNIVERSE CREATION WEEK

"IN THE BEGINNING"

"LET THERE BE LIGHT"

GENESIS 1:1

UCW DAY 1 | UCW DAY 2 | UCW DAY 3 | UCW DAY 4 | UCW DAY 5

GENESIS 1:3

UCW DAY 6

1 2 3 4 5 6
ECW DAYS

EARTH CREATION WEEK

In the following illustration, I show this concept in the same format as our previous models, so that the strong similarities can be clearly seen:

WEEK WITHIN A WEEK CREATION MODEL
UNIVERSE CREATION WEEK

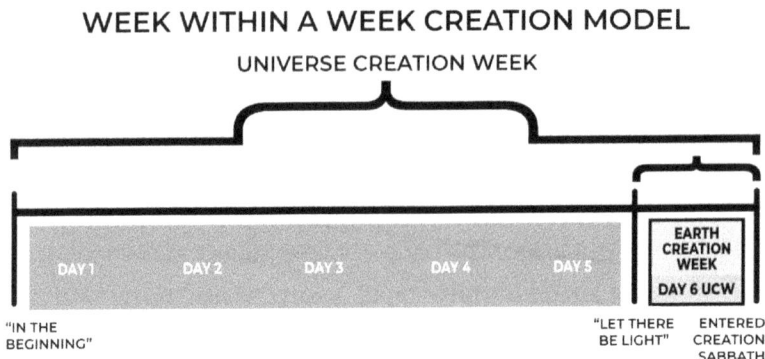

					EARTH CREATION WEEK
DAY 1	DAY 2	DAY 3	DAY 4	DAY 5	DAY 6 UCW

"IN THE BEGINNING"   "LET THERE BE LIGHT"   ENTERED CREATION SABBATH

In the next chapters, we will look at all the distinct days of creation in much greater detail. For now, the important point is merely that there are two different weeks of six days found in the creation account in Genesis, and that the ECW is a week within the UCW.

To elaborate on this overlapping structure, both weeks have the same theme (creation) and follow the same pattern of other six-days-and-sabbath weeks already discussed.

The sixth day of the Universe Creation Week (UCW) and the Earth Creation Week (ECW) both ended once Adam and Eve were created. This means that both cycles have a sabbath day that started at the same time, matching the pattern of wilderness cycles which both terminated simultaneously when the Israelites entered the Promised Land. It's also like Daniel's prophecy of seventy weeks, in that the last week is a subset of the total. In this case, the weeks also terminate at the same time.

When reading the creation account, it might seem natural to assume that the light God commanded into existence in Genesis 1:3 is the same light which many presume to be associated with the Big Bang at the time of the universe's creation. That seems logical. The universe is mass, mass is energy, and energy is light, and lots of it. The Big Bang plus energy release plus the creation of the universe results in *"Let there be light."*

However, I don't believe this is exactly what God is saying. The whole truth is counterintuitive, which is why this matter has been shrouded for centuries by a veil of thick clouds like those that hid the sun's early light from the Earth all those billions of years ago.

The thesis of this book is that the light which God commanded into existence in Genesis 1:2 is the light that first broke through the clouds onto the Earth. The Earth was God's frame of reference when he spoke. This is the moment of the Earth's first dawn, a different light event than the one which may have occurred at the commencement of space and time at the very beginning.

To recap, God said that he created the heavens and the Earth. This is what I suggest he did in the first five days of the UCW, before the start of the ECW. From this perspective, *"in the beginning"* refers to everything he created from day one to day five of the UCW. Everything that had already been created in Genesis 1:1, such as the stars and galaxies, our solar system, and the Earth, in its primordial state, were included in those things which had been created *"in the beginning."* After that point in time, the Earth Creation Week Cycle commenced, once God gave the Word.

Let's now go back through time, starting at the moment God first created the universe, which defines the start of the UCW approximately thirteen billion years ago.

Then we fast-forward approximately eleven billion years. By this time, the universe had massively expanded and matured. God had established the Earth in its position in our solar system, and our moon in orbit around it. The Earth was covered by water but was otherwise virtually uninhabitable. At this time, the Spirit of God was hovering over the Earth, which was already spinning on its axis. He looked upon the sea and the Earth just as a gardener or landscaper would, considering how he would transform this rough clump of celestial clay into a beautiful garden upon which man could dwell.

This is when God initiated the Genesis narrative concerning the Earth Creation Week, starting in Genesis 1:2.

In conclusion, I believe that the week-within-a-week creation model provides a significant and profound new perspective of the Genesis narrative. As I will show, this structure opens the door to finding a rational and effective basis for quantifying the length of days in Genesis. It also provides a framework which allows the creation narrative to be reconciled with science.

In the following chapters, I will discuss these subjects in detail. For now, we can see from the scorecard that this theory checks all the boxes required.

EVALUATION SCORECARD

✓	✓	✓	✓	✓
SCRIPTURALLY SUPPORTED	AGREES WITH SCIENCE	PLAUSIBLE 'DAYS' OF DEFINED LENGTH	AFFIRMS GOD IS CREATOR	INTERNAL INTEGRITY

Seventeen

THE HARD NUMBERS

> Teach us to number our days, that we may gain a
> heart of wisdom. (Psalm 90:12)

BEFORE PRESENTING THE length of days in each creation week, I will review some relevant principles already established at this point in our discussion.

- Several scriptures compare a thousand years to being like a day for God.
- God's prophetic year consists of 360 days.
- There are several six-days-and-sabbath weeks.
- These weeks have different durations.

Keeping these principles in mind, recall the Kabbalists' attempt to calculate the length of God's days in creation. They presumed that a day was a thousand years, a year was 365.25 days, and a day was part of a seven-thousand-year week. As we learned, the Kabbalists suggested that a divine creation day was 2.56 billion years long. Based on this calculation, they then speculated that the age of the universe should be six times 2.56 billion years, or 15.36 billion years old.

As noted earlier, I believe this theory has some serious problems. First, accepting these calculations would mean accepting that plants, created on day three, had their origins ten billion years ago. The Earth, as well as the universe, would presumably be 15.36 billion years old. Neither of these scenarios is supported by science.

Although I feel we must reject the conclusions of Kabbalist theory, its efforts do perhaps represent the start of a productive line of thinking. If we develop this idea using the premises we have established in previous chapters, I believe we can find a way to calculate the length of a "day" that conforms to modern scientific findings.

To start, let's consider 2 Peter 3:8: *"But do not forget this one thing, dear friends: With the Lord a day is like a thousand years, and a thousand years are like a day."* One might wonder, of all the things that were going on in the early church, why would Peter exhort believers not to forget this one thing about a day being like a thousand years? Why is it important?

To figure that out, let's return to the four fundamental principles listed at the beginning of this chapter. By applying them, perhaps we can derive some answers.

If we know that a day with the Lord is like a thousand years, and a prophetic year of God is 360 days, then it follows that one day with the Lord is 1,000 times 360 days, or 360,000 human days. And if a thousand years are also like a day to God, then 360,000 days would be equal to 360,000 times 1,000 years (of 360 days). When we multiply these numbers of days, and express the solution in years, we get 360 million years.

I suggest that this biblically derived unit of time provides a plausible basis for the use of the word "day" in Genesis, as applied to creation. I believe this approach has several merits and I will use it as the basis for the timeline of this book's model.

However, we can validate this concept in a more basic way in order to provide additional assurance that the overall framework of our suggested timeframes is sound.

If we take the full 13.8-billion-year age of the universe and divide it by six, we derive 2.3 billion years per day in the Universe Creation Week. If we then divide 2.3 billion years into the six days of the Earth Creation Week, it yields days that are 383.3 million years long. This means that both methods generate Earth creation days in the range of 360 and 384 million years in length.

We recall the biblical precedents involving cycles which can appear in multiple timeframes of each other, such as the wilderness model (multiples of forty) and the example from Daniel's prophecy of seventy weeks.

Below we will recap these numbers and relationships. The table is based on a 360-million-year Earth creation day. There are six of these days in the Earth Creation Week for a total of 2.16 billion years (six times 360 million).

Six creation days are also the length of one day in the Universe Creation Week. Therefore, one universe creation day is 2.16 billion years long and six universe creation days total 12.96 billion years (six times 2.16 billion).

THE CONVERSION MULTIPLES

Biblical Days and Years:

1 prophetic year of God equals:	360 days
'1000 years is like a day' would be:	1000 x 360 days or 360,000 days
'A day is like a 1000 years' would be:	1000 x 360 days x 360,000 equals 360 million years or one creation day

Earth Creation Week conversion multiples:

1 Earth creation day equals:	360 million years
6 Earth creation days would be:	6 x 360,000,000 equals 2.16 billion years

Universe Creation Week conversion multiples:

1 Universe creation day equals:	2.16 billion years
6 Universe creation days would be:	6 x 2.16 billion equals 12.96 billion years

This model projects that the Universe Creation Week began 12.96 billion years ago. In Chapter Twenty, I will discuss the age of the universe in detail and provide two plausible arguments that fully reconcile the scientific age of the universe (13.8 billion years) and this 12.96-billion-year timeframe.

Using the numbers from the preceding chart, the next illustration shows the relative timeframes of the two creation week cycles, in which the Earth Creation Week is a subset (a week within a week) of the Universe Creation Week:

UNIVERSE CREATION WEEK

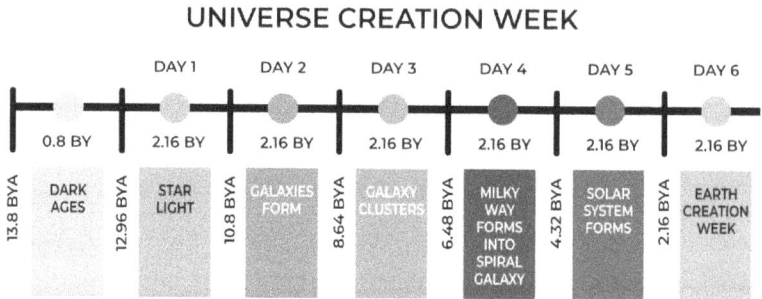

In the other six-days-and-sabbath patterns we've looked at, the days are of equal length. Therefore, it seems very important that each of the creation days of both creation weeks be of equal length.

We can see this is the case in the illustration above.

As discussed in Chapter Five, the use of the number seven is significant. Its associated meanings of perfection and completion would be lost if there weren't seven actual days. Both of these factors lend credibility to the thesis that there are indeed six equally divided days in each of the creation weeks, plus a sabbath day.

I think it's also important to note that my calculations for the length of the Earth creation days are based only on biblical references specifically related to what days and years mean to God, such as 2 Peter 3:8. This means that the length of these days aren't randomly selected but rather directly supported by scripture.

Now that we've established the timeframes for the two creation weeks, let us compare the structure of the week-within-a-week creation model with the previous models, taking note that they all display a "within" characteristic similar to the creation model:

WEEK WITHIN A WEEK CREATION MODEL

UCW 12.96 BILLION YEARS

ECW

2.16 BY

10.8 BILLION YEARS

| DAY 1 | DAY 2 | DAY 3 | DAY 4 | DAY 5 | DAY 6 |

"IN THE BEGINNING"

"LET THERE BE LIGHT"

ENTERED CREATION SABBATH

WILDERNESS MODEL

440 YEARS

40 YEARS SINAI WILDERNESS

400 YEARS WILDERNESS CAPTIVITY

START OF EGYPT CAPTIVITY

THE EXODUS

ENTERED PROMISED LAND

DANIEL'S PROPHECY MODEL

70 WEEKS

69 WEEKS OF 7 YEARS/WEEK WITH 360 DAYS/YEAR = 173,880 DAYS

2000-YEAR CHURCH GAP

1 WEEK OF 7 YEARS (70TH WEEK)

START OF 70 WEEKS

CHRIST'S FIRST COMING

ENTER MILLENNIUM

And then there is also the battle of Jericho model, which I show again below. For comparison purposes, I also show a slightly modified version of the week-within-a-week creation model to highlight the striking similarities between the two:

WEEK WITHIN A WEEK CREATION MODEL
UCW 12.96 BILLION YEARS

					ECW
		10.8 BILLION YEARS			2.16 BY
DAY 1	DAY 2	DAY 3	DAY 4	DAY 5	DAY 6

"IN THE BEGINNING" "LET THERE BE LIGHT" ENTERED CREATION SABBATH

BATTLE OF JERICHO MODEL
7 DAYS

						7 MARCHES
		6 MARCHES AROUND JERICHO				
DAY 1	DAY 2	DAY 3	DAY 4	DAY 5	DAY 6	DAY 7

START OF JERICHO SIEGE START OF SABBATH ENTERED JERICHO

It could be argued that the Jericho model offers the best comparison to the Creation Week Model because its sabbath day is itself divided into equal smaller sections, just like the Earth creation days. The Jericho model also takes the form of a sabbath week, mirroring the creation week and clearly demonstrating a week-within-a-week structure. In addition, and in my opinion, the marches (revolutions) around the city can be seen as analogous to the celestial orbit of the Earth around the sun, thus tying this model even more closely to the creation week.

It can be seen from the above comparison that these models share exactly the same structure: there is a wilderness within a wilderness, a week within the seventy weeks, and finally a week of marches within the week of marches. The last component of each model is a subset of the total structure and shares the same theme. The last component ends at the same time as the larger cycle and all these models result in entering either God's rest or the Promised Land.

This analysis demonstrates that the week-within-a-week creation model is based on sound biblical examples and principles.

In this chapter, I have presented the case for considering the Earth creation days and universe creation days to be of different lengths. I have also shown that a UCW day is equal in length to six days of the ECW.

The week-within-a-week creation model and its timeframes provide a completely new framework through which the Genesis narrative can be understood. In addition, the brief comparison between the Genesis week and natural history which I have outlined above demonstrates a remarkable alignment between the two.

In the next chapter, I will examine this comparison in more detail.

Eighteen

THE EARTH CREATION WEEK TIMELINE

> It was you who set the boundaries of the earth; you
> made both summer and winter. (Psalm 74:17)

IF THE THESIS of this book is correct, the development of the Earth
and life as recorded in the natural history of our planet should align
with the timing predicted by the week-within-a-week creation model.
Below, you will find a table that lays out the creative acts of God on
each creation day and when those days commenced, as recorded in
the Bible. I have also included the scientific record result associated
with each respective day.

You can see that the timeline of natural history on the Earth is
consistent with the timeline of my ECW model. For example, land
vertebrates and mammals appear in the fossil record approximately
360 million years ago, in agreement with the ECW's sixth day. Fish
appeared more than five hundred million years ago, within the range
of the ECW's fifth day.

Incidentally, the Cambrian explosion of life occurred on ECW
day five. Most of the animal life which appeared in the Cambrian
explosion was aquatic, which is also in tune with this model of the
Genesis days.[55]

CREATION WEEK TIMELINE

EARTH CREATION CYCLE	INITIATIVE	RESULT	TIME FRAME
4.5 billion years ago	Earth without form	Tectonic, volcanic activity Great oxygenation event	Partway in UCW day 5
2.16 billion years ago	Earth in dark, watery state	Earth still uninhabitable	End of UCW Day 5
DAY 1 2.16 billion years ago	God commands light	Significant vapourization Additional oxygenation	Start of ECW Day 1. Start of UCW Day 6 360 m. yrs.
DAY 2 1.8 billion years ago	God commands waters part	Oxygenation of air Vapourization	360 m. yrs. duration
DAY 3 1.44 billion years ago	Dry land and plant formation	More oxygenation/sky clears. Tectonic activity	360 m. yrs. duration
DAY 4 1.08 billion years ago	Sun, moon and stars appear	Air, sun and plants provide the conditions for diverse life	360 m. yrs. duration
DAY 5 720 million years ago	Birds and fish appear	Eco system developing Cambrian explosion of life	360 m. yrs. duration
DAY 6 360 million years ago	Animals, vertebrates appear	Full eco system in place man created very late day 6	360 m. yrs. duration
DAY 7 4000 BC	Creation Sabbath Day	No new life creation	End of ECW Day 6 End of UCW Day 6

The next chart contains additional details pertaining to the developments which occurred on each of the days of creation and how they match up with my creation week model.[56]

EARTH CREATION WEEK MODEL
VS. NATURAL HISTORY

EARTH CREATION DAY	YEARS AGO	EVENTS IN NATURAL HISTORY
	4.5 billion years ago	**ARCHAEAN EON** Moon collision/creation. Earth molten magma. Planet started to cool and heavy elements sink into earth. Atmosphere mostly hydrogen and helium. Constant volcanic eruptions pumped ammonia and carbon dioxide into the atmosphere. Atmospheric composition like Venus and Mars. Great oxygenation event began 2.4 billion years ago. Sun was 30% dimmer than now.
START ECW **DAY 1**	2.16 billion years ago	**PALEOPROTEROZOIC ERA** Atmosphere becomes more oxygenated; oxygen makes up 10% of atmosphere. Methane abundant in atmosphere. Aerobic eukaryotes present. Oxygen helps to create ozone layer.
START ECW **DAY 2**	1.8 billion years ago	**PROTEROZOIC EON** Ocean basins close due to plate tectonics. Super-continent formation. Increased oxygenation of atmosphere.
START ECW **DAY 3**	1.44 billion years ago	**MESOPROTEROZOIC ERA** Eukaryotes give rise to fungi and plants. Increased photosynthesis and oxygenation.
START ECW **DAY 4**	1.08 billion years ago	**NEOPROTEROZOIC ERA** Sun becomes brighter and more visible. Increased plant life. Super continents start to break up. Increased oxygen.
START ECW **DAY 5**	720 million years ago	**CAMBRIAN ERA** 538 mya: Aquatic life created in Cambrian Explosion. Appearance of most animal phyla within 20-30 million years. 600 mya: First skeletal elements. 550 mya: First fish. 450 mya: Sudden diversification of metazoan families. 400 mya: First jawed fish. 400 mya: First amphibians.

EARTH CREATION WEEK MODEL VS. NATURAL HISTORY CON'T

EARTH CREATION DAY	YEARS AGO	EVENTS IN NATURAL HISTORY
START ECW **DAY 6**	**360 million years ago**	350 mya: First reptiles. 240 mya: First dinosaurs. 65 mya: Dinosaurs extinction. 220 mya: First mammals. 100 mya: First primates. 50 mya: Mammal diversification. 2 - 5 mya: First hominids. 300 kya: First Homo sapiens.

Based on this model, day one of the ECW started 2.16 billion years ago. Prior to that, the Earth was in a molten and uninhabitable condition.

As you can see, this model appears to be very accurate in terms of how it lines up with the geologic history of the Earth. The increase in oxygen in the atmosphere over hundreds of millions of years created the potential for life. The dates strongly match the appearance of fish, animals, and Homo sapiens in the fossil record.

In the next chapter, we will see that this model's projections are also remarkably harmonized with the measured age of the universe. This overall correlation serves to validate the division of time generated by our model.

That being said, Genesis 1:11 does say that plants in all their various kinds were produced on day three. While the very first plant life does appear on day three of our model, the fossil records show that most plants first appeared five hundred million years ago. This would put the majority of plants firmly in the scope of day five.

However, evolutionary biologist Blair Hedges and his team have found that "land plants and fungi evolved much earlier than previously thought."[57] They discovered that land plants had emerged by about seven hundred million years ago and land fungi by about 1.3 billion years ago. This would put the first development of photosynthesis within the range of the ECW's third day, with the continuation of plant development occurring from there.

Furthermore, Therese Sallstedt of the Swedish Museum of Natural History has discovered fossilized red algae that she dates to 1.6 billion years old.[58]

In addition, *New Scientist* magazine reported in February 2020 that billion-year-old seaweed fossils had been discovered in China.[59]

All this evidence supports the proposed model and its timeframe for the appearance of plants.

The appearance of plants helped lower the temperature of the Earth's surface and create an environment suitable for animals. The conditions for plant life were present on day three due to the availability of oxygenated air, the appearance of land, and the translucent light of the sun through the clouds.

God's creation of new types of plants continued into day four as the sunlight became visible. The full scope of plants, vegetation, and fruit-bearing trees could only fully develop as the sun's light became directly visible. Thus, the scope of work which started on day three continued through days four and five. It at least seems safe to say that plant life preceded the creation of other life.

Plants were the first in God's initiative in biogenesis, the process by which life comes from other life. It was the first form of speciation, with plants reproducing after their own kind.

This ordering of events agrees with our model. John F. McCarthy comments on St. Augustine's writings and provides further context:

> In St. Augustine's view, the text of Genesis is saying that in the beginning the ground received from God the (passive) power to produce plants, so that the things that would come into being over the spread of time were, so to speak, in the ground as in the "roots of the ages.[60]

God reveals that the next important milestone was the sun becoming directly visible on day four, making additional plant life viable. In my view, there is overlap in the scope of work for the creation days just as there is overlap in the work done at a cabin on the weekend, as discussed earlier. There is no need for God to repeat that he continued to create plants on days four and five. The plant creation process, which started on day three, was followed by the creation of the full variety of plant life which occurred as conditions on the Earth allowed.

Finally, it's important to keep in mind the very few words God used in the creation narrative to describe the vast processes and creative activity which spanned billions of years. We must leave room for some unknowns.

Another such uncertainty is the timeline for the appearance of birds. Genesis 1:21 tells us that birds were created on day five. In my proposed model, the fifth day spans the period from 720 million years ago to 360 million years ago. Based on this theory, that's when birds should have first appeared. However, the oldest discovered bird fossils are approximately 160 million years old.

I cannot offer a conclusive explanation for this anomaly. However, we do note something interesting and perhaps relevant in regard to birds: based on several key anatomical features, birds are scientifically categorized as dinosaurs. These features include skull formation, beta-keratin scales and feathers, teeth composition, and bone structures. These features are shared by all archosaurs, a category which includes reptiles, dinosaurs, and birds. In fact, birds are archosaurs.[61]

This broad categorization opens the door for a broader interpretation of birds appearing on day five.

We briefly expand on this theory related to the appearance of birds and dinosaurs in Appendix Two. Interested readers can judge for themselves its validity and sufficiency.

Ultimately, some mysteries will remain, but it can be seen that the framework of this model matches the record of natural history very well. That is, the vast majority of geologic events and appearances of life align closely with these predictions.

I would also point out that by day five, God had created the sea, the sky, and the land. Plant life had already commenced. This means that the environment was ready to be filled with new forms of life, like fish and birds. In this context, God explains in very few words how his creative acts are related to each other and the environment.

Let's return to our cabin analogy. Once the framing of an extension has been finished, the next step is sheathing the exterior walls and wiring the inside for electricity. We can think of both jobs as occurring on a particular "day" even if they don't get finished the next day, or even the next week. The scope of work is defined partly by the structure under consideration, not just by the time it takes to complete it.

In a similar way, I believe God uses the scope of related work, combined with linear time, in his Genesis narrative. He is using the full breadth of the meaning of work in this way.

We must allow for God's creative license. We also need to guard against the inclination to perceive his creative work in overly simplistic ways. Creation was a vastly complicated process that took place over billions of years, even though God chose to reveal it through a very simple and concise narrative. In this way, anyone reading his account could benefit and gain a fundamental understanding of who the Creator is and his relationship with us, which is its ultimate purpose.

For example, around 252 million years ago the Earth experienced the Permian extinction, an event during which upwards of ninety percent of aquatic life became extinct.[62]

Creation was therefore not a one-and-done event; it was a process marked by creation and destruction. A number of extinction events on the Earth caused massive changes to biodiversity, allowed for the formation of fossil fuels, and also made new creation possible.

To further illustrate the principle of destruction and re-creation, we can again consider the nation of Israel, which was also God's creation. Isaiah 43:1–2 says, *"But now, this is what the Lord says—he who created you, Jacob, he who formed you, Israel…"* The history of Israel is one of formation, prosperity, judgment, and destruction. Israel was reduced to only a remnant of itself many times as it underwent persecution, enslavement, wilderness experiences, displacement, and regathering. For Israel, God was like a master gardener, pruning the branches and turning over the soil, all to produce a nation that pleased him and through whom he could accomplish all his purposes.

In the same way, God's creation on the Earth underwent destruction and reformation many times. As a result, the face of the Earth, its geology and its lifeforms, were changed. Thus, the picture of the Earth's history aligns with how God has been seen to work in the Bible. Out of destruction, new creation is made.

In summary, the 360-million-year length of each creation day proposed by this model was derived using biblical patterns and scriptures related to time. In my view, it also provides the possible best fit with the Genesis account. In these ways, it stands on its own merit. I do allow for an element of mystery, given the many complexities, vast amount of time involved in the process of creation, and few words used to explain it all.

Based on the foregoing, I pose three questions:

1. Does the week-within-a-week creation model generate a division of time that adequately meets my suggested biblical definition of the word "day"?
2. Does the equal length of days provided by this model enable a plausible interpretation of the word "day" as required by the evaluation criteria?

3. Does the timeline created by this thesis match up well against the natural history of the Earth?

My assessment is that the answer to all these questions is "Yes." Accordingly, I believe that the Earth Creation Week model meets all evaluation criteria.

EVALUATION SCORECARD

✓	✓	✓	✓	✓
SCRIPTURALLY SUPPORTED	AGREES WITH SCIENCE	PLAUSIBLE 'DAYS' OF DEFINED LENGTH	AFFIRMS GOD IS CREATOR	INTERNAL INTEGRITY

Nineteen

AGE OF THE UNIVERSE

> Some have asserted that the universe was self-generated. This violates, however, a primary law of logic: the law of non-contradiction that says the universe cannot be itself and the thing it creates at the same time.[63] —Charles Colson

IN CHAPTER SIXTEEN, I introduced the week-within-a-week creation model and its related timeline. If you recall, this model proposes that the days of the Earth Creation Week are each 360 million years long, with the six days of this week totalling 2.16 billion years (six times 360 million).

I also postulated that the days of the Universe Creation Week are each 2.16 billion years long, with the six days of this week totalling 12.96 billion years (six times 2.16 billion). This implies that the model estimates the total length of the UCW, and therefore the age of the universe, to be 12.96 billion years.

So how well do the timeframes of this model compare to the actual age of the universe? We know from astronomy that the current estimate of the age of the universe is 13.8 billion years. This gives us a 93.9 percent match with the best scientific theory today (12.96 divided by 13.8).

This theory is in the general ballpark of being accurate, although these two numbers are still eight hundred million years apart. Is there a way to bring them closer together?

I think there is.

I will now review the methodologies which astronomers use to determine the age of the universe. I want to emphasize that I'm not questioning the scientific methodologies currently in use. But I do feel it's important to appreciate all the nuances and margins of error related to this subject. They may have a significant bearing on the efforts to reconcile the results of these two independent approaches.

Astronomers and astrophysicists employ two principal methods to determine the age of the universe. One involves studying old stars, while the other measures the speed of the expansion of the universe.

The methodology for dating stars involves determining their brightness, their distance from the Earth, and their metallicity.[64] Metallicity measures the relative amounts of elements found in a star that are heavier than hydrogen. The older the star, the more hydrogen is converted to heavier metals.

This measurement is accomplished through spectral analysis. In order to estimate the age of the star being studied, the spectral analysis is compared to models of the nuclear reactions expected to occur within stars of various sizes, brightness, and other factors. Because this methodology depends on models to interpret data, its estimates have a higher range of error.

For example, there is a star found in the Milky Way galaxy (HD140283) that has been nicknamed the Methuselah star, after the long-lived Methuselah of Genesis. This star was thus named because to date it is the oldest star to be discovered and is calculated to be 14.46 billion years old.[65]

This number has raised questions, because the best estimate of the age of the universe is 13.8 billion, give or take 0.2 billion years. The question then is how this star can be older than the universe.

The current explanation for this anomaly is that the range of error for the measurement of the age of Methuselah is 0.8 billion years. In other words, it might only be 13.6 billion years old.

The other method used for aging the universe is measuring the speed of the expansion of the universe. Since there are several independent ways to arrive at this measurement, scientists have a greater level of confidence in the estimates obtained.

This speed of expansion is known as the Hubble constant. It's not a constant in the sense that never changes. It's a constant in the sense that once this number is determined, it allows for a precise calculation of the age of the universe. Hubble's Law is the observation that galaxies are moving away from the Earth at speeds proportional to their distance. The farther away they are, the faster they are moving.

A basic way to understand the concept of the Hubble constant is to compare it to a common formula:

distance = rate x time

If you're driving to a location sixty kilometres away, and you're travelling at sixty kilometres per hour, it will take you one hour to arrive at your destination (60 kilometres = 60 kilometres per hour x 1 hour).

If, however, you decide to travel at 120 kilometres per hour, twice as fast, you will arrive at your destination in only thirty minutes.

To solve for time, you divide the distance by the speed of travel, as follows:

$T = d \div r$

In this formula, because r (speed) is the denominator, the larger the number (r), the lower the solution T (time) will be.

The same principle applies to the formula which uses the Hubble constant to calculate the age of the universe. The higher the speed at which the universe is expanding (the Hubble constant), the less time it would have taken for the universe to have expanded to where it is today. So the higher the Hubble constant (higher speed of expansion), the lower the age of the universe.

The best estimate for the value of the Hubble constant is seventy-one kilometres per second per megaparsec, one megaparsec being equal to three million lightyears. This is equivalent to a speed of seventy-one thousand kilometres per second, or approximately twenty-four percent of the speed of light. Using this value for the Hubble constant yields an age of 13.77 billion years for the universe.[66]

Estimates for the Hubble constant have been refined over the past number of years.[67] In 2010, it was estimated to be seventy-three plus/minus two—in other words, in the range of seventy-one to seventy-five.

In 2022, *Astrophysical Journal* reported that researchers used the Hubble telescope to arrive at an estimate of seventy-three kilometres per second plus/minus one. Other studies have arrived at estimates which are below seventy.[68]

Given these variables, let's now turn to examining how our model can be reconciled to these age measurements for the universe.

RECONCILIATION THEORY ONE

We know that using a Hubble constant of seventy-one yields an age of 13.77 billion years. For the sake of illustration, if you assume a Hubble constant of seventy-four—a value within the error range estimate reported by *Astrophysical Journal*—you will derive an age of the universe of 13.21 billion years old. Based on an age of 13.21 billion years, our model's age of 12.96 billion years would represent a 98.1 percent agreement.

We can also arrive at the length of a day in the ECW based on a normal year of 365.25 days instead of the biblical prophetic year of 360 days. In this case, the calculation for a day would be 365.25 times 1,000 times 1,000, or 365,250,000 years. This translates to an ECW of 2.1915 billion years (six times 365.255 million) and a UCW of 13.149 billion years (six times 2.1915 billion). This gives us a 99.84 percent agreement with the age of the universe based on a Hubble constant of seventy-four. Based on the accepted estimate of 13.77 billion, it would still mean a 95.49 percent agreement.

But there is yet another possible explanation.

RECONCILIATION THEORY TWO

There is a natural assumption that the Universe Creation Week cycle began exactly at the same time as the Big Bang, when the universe first started to expand.

But are they really aligned that closely? I think there is a strong argument to be made that this is not the case.

Recall that the Earth Creation Week cycle commenced when God said, *"Let there be light"* (Genesis 1:3). Therefore, this cycle could not have begun at the moment the Earth was first formed. As we have discussed, the Earth was already in existence, in orbit around the sun and covered with water, when God issued his command. The Earth at that time was covered in darkness. The appearance of the sun's light initiated the Earth Creation Week cycle.

This brings us to a discussion of modern theories on the origins of the universe. NASA Science explains:

> Around 13.8 billion years ago, the universe expanded faster than the speed of light for a fraction of a second, a period called cosmic inflation. Scientists aren't sure what came before inflation or what powered it. It's possible that energy during this period

was just part of the fabric of space-time. When this cosmic inflation stopped, the energy driving it transferred to matter and light, the big bang.[69]

Within minutes of the Big Bang, hydrogen, helium, and other trace elements had formed. Approximately 380,000 years after the Big Bang, the universe had cooled enough that protons and neutrons could combine into ionized atoms of hydrogen and helium. The formation of these first atoms created a cosmic microwave background that can still be observed in the universe today. The Max Planck Institute for Astronomy have "timed the end of the epoch of reionisation of the neutral hydrogen gas to about 1.1 billion years after the Big Bang."[70]

Similar, an article in *Astronomy* explains that early in the history of the universe, there was a cosmic dark age:

> The cosmic dark ages were a time in which the universe was enveloped by a fog of neutral hydrogen that trapped the light of the first stars and galaxies. The fog didn't lift until 1 billion years after the Big Bang.[71]

It is believed that UV light was necessary to cause this reionization of the universe and that the source of this UV light was early stars or quasars.[72]

To summarize what we're being told by astronomers: there was a period of complete darkness in the universe for upwards of a billion years after the Big Bang. This paints a darkness-to-light picture which closely parallels the conditions on the Earth described by the Bible before the commencement of the Earth Creation Week.

For this reason, I believe that the Universe Creation Week actually began when the light from the stars in the heavens first became visible.

Wouldn't you like to have been there at that time? Suddenly, the lights went on. Starlight penetrated the blackness of deep space, shining a spotlight on the new creation, thus ending the cosmic dark ages.

This is what I believe happened. My interpretation is consistent with the biblical precedent of the Earth Creation Week. As we will see in Chapter Twenty-Six, this theory is also consistent with a number of other darkness-to-light cycles we have identified in the Bible.

Furthermore, this provides the basis for another plausible reconciliation between the established age of the universe and the Universe Creation Week. Using the current estimated age of the universe of 13.77 billion years, subtract the duration of time that the universe was enveloped in darkness, approximately eight hundred million years. We can see that 13.77 billion less 0.8 billion is equal to 12.97. Compare this to the Bible-based projection of 12.96 billion years. Such a comparison yields a hypothetical agreement of nearly one hundred percent.

Frankly, we can't know these things for certain. Even today, astrophysicists are perfecting their estimates of the Hubble constant. Who knows exactly how long the dark ages lasted?

But both reconciliation approaches have at least the potential to provide a plausible and perfect alignment of the week-within-a-week creation model with the measurements of science. This potential alignment is really quite incredible and serves to strengthen my case.

MORE ABOUT THE UNIVERSE

Amazing as all this may seem, there is more. We know from astronomers that before the Big Bang there was a period of cosmic inflation—that is, the fabric of space expanded for a fraction of a second faster than the speed of light. We also know that science has no explanation for how or why this occurred.

Perhaps scripture can provide insight. Consider the following verses:

He alone stretches out the heavens… (Job 9:8)

The Lord, who stretches out the heavens… (Zachariah 12:1)

He stretches out the heavens like a canopy, and spreads them out like a tent to live in. (Isaiah 40:22)

Do these scriptures refer to the expansion of the universe? I believe they do. If I'm right, how would the authors of the Bible know the universe was expanding when this was observed by scientists for the first time only in the early part of the twentieth century? In my view, the fact that this concept is presented many times throughout the Bible clearly reflects its importance. I believe this possibility is worth mentioning here as it lends support to the overall belief that the Bible is remarkable and trustworthy.

We should also keep in mind Newton's first law of thermodynamics, which states that energy cannot be created nor destroyed.[73] This law therefore creates a puzzle, as the initial source of the energy behind an expanding universe and all the matter and energy it contains is not known. The explanation found in the Bible is that this energy came from God.

This chapter has presented a plausible model for aligning the creation narrative in Genesis with astronomy and should encourage us by reinforcing that we are on the right track.

In the next chapter, I will look at the possible order of events occurring during the Universe Creation Week.

Twenty

UNIVERSE CREATION WEEK

Do you know the law of the heavens? Can you set
up God's dominion over the earth? (Job 38:33)

IN THE LAST chapter, I presented my theory that the Universe Creation Week lasted for 12.96 billion years and consisted of six days,
each 2.16 billion years in length. Each UCW day was associated
with God's creative involvement in the development of all celestial
components of the heavens.

Prior to the start of the UCW, and aligning with science, there
was a cosmic dark age. Specifically, 0.8 billion years of the cosmic
dark age plus the UCW's 12.96 billion years equals 13.8 billion years.

I provide below a visual representation that illustrates the potential creative involvement of God on each of these six days.

UNIVERSE CREATION WEEK

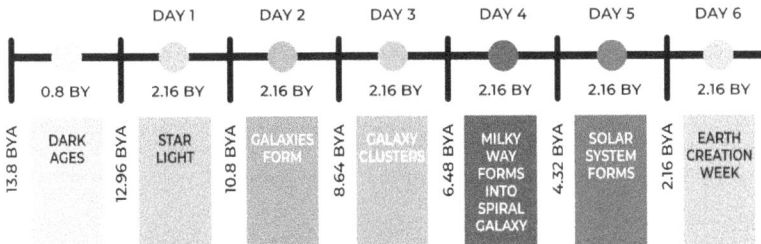

	DAY 1	DAY 2	DAY 3	DAY 4	DAY 5	DAY 6
0.8 BY	2.16 BY	2.16 BY	2.16 BY	2.16 BY	2.16 BY	2.16 BY
13.8 BYA — DARK AGES	12.96 BYA — STAR LIGHT	10.8 BYA — GALAXIES FORM	8.64 BYA — GALAXY CLUSTERS	6.48 BYA — MILKY WAY FORMS INTO SPIRAL GALAXY	4.32 BYA — SOLAR SYSTEM FORMS	2.16 BYA — EARTH CREATION WEEK

God, for reasons we cannot know, didn't provide a creation narrative for the universe in the same way he provided one for the creation of the Earth.

However, based on the timeline of the development of the universe, I wish to present a hypothetical narrative of these events as God might have told it had he chosen to do so. I have used the same format as Genesis 1, trying my best to accurately depict what I think could have happened over the course of those six workdays. As I go, I will provide some brief explanations and actual scriptures to support my proposed version of events.

> The Spirit of God was hovering over the darkness of the heavens (the dark ages): and God said, "Let there be light."
>
> And there was light. (Stars started to shine due to reionization.) And there was evening and there was morning, the first day.
>
> And God said, "Let the stars in all their vast array increase in number and give their light and fill the whole heavens. And let the stars gather to make greater lights in the heavens. (Early galaxy formation: "Can you bring forth the constellations in their seasons...?" [Job 38:31])
>
> And there was evening and morning, the second day.
>
> And God said, "Let the greater lights increase in abundance and let them gather in all manner and fill the heavens." (Galaxies cluster together due to gravity.)
>
> And there was evening and morning, the third day.

And God said, "Let the greater lights spin like a wheel, with arms that reach to the heavens." (The Milky Way becomes a spiral galaxy.)

And there was evening and morning, the fourth day.

And God said, "Let the Earth and the Moon and the Sun bind together and let the Sun and the Moon give their light upon the darkness of the Earth and upon the waters. (The Earth's solar system formed, including proto-Earth; waters started to cover the earth: *"The earth takes shape like clay under a seal"* [Job 38:14], *"Who shut up the sea behind doors when it burst forth from the womb..."* [Job 38:8])

And there was evening and there was morning, the fifth day.

Then we reach the moment of Genesis 1:2:

And the Spirit of God was hovering over the deep, and God said, "Let there be light. And there was light.

And there was evening and there was morning, the first day."

(This marks the beginning of day six of the UCW, and the beginning and end of day one of the ECW.)

In summary, this model fits closely with the age of the universe and provides a plausible length of days. It doesn't contradict data from the field of astronomy. Therefore, the Universe Creation Week model meets all the evaluation criteria.

EVALUATION SCORECARD

✓	✓	✓	✓	✓
SCRIPTURALLY SUPPORTED	AGREES WITH SCIENCE	PLAUSIBLE 'DAYS' OF DEFINED LENGTH	AFFIRMS GOD IS CREATOR	INTERNAL INTEGRITY

Twenty-One

ADAM, ISRAEL, AND JESUS

> ...for you, Israel, are my servant. I have made you,
> you are my servant... (Isaiah 44:21)

THE PURPOSE OF this book is to provide a reasonable and plausible explanation of how a literal reading of scripture can be aligned with modern science. Given the importance of Adam and Eve to the Christian faith, the biblical narrative that introduces them needs to be reconciled with the findings of modern anthropology.

As with the creation narrative, I will use biblical patterns and principles as well as logic in the effort to provide this full reconciliation. The thesis presented will be subject to the same evaluation scorecard.

Recall that as a first requirement, any viable model must be supported by scripture. I believe that this includes the narrative about Adam and Eve because it sets up an indispensable theological foundation for the whole Bible. Without a real Adam and Eve, the Bible could be seen as fallible and allegorical.

Furthermore, Christian theology is built upon the need for a redemptive plan by God due to the sin of Adam and Eve. In the New Testament, Christ is actually referred to as *"the last Adam"* (1

Corinthians 15:45) and his lineage in Luke 3:38 is traced right back to *"Adam, the son of God."*

In summary, in order to be valid according to my criteria, an acceptable theory must affirm that Adam was an actual person.

When I began my analysis of the creation account, I also stipulated that the findings of modern science be affirmed. This includes studies on the timeframes of human origins. So any theory concerning Adam that doesn't affirm current scientific understandings related to anthropology will be rejected.

I believe it is important to first recognize some key associations between Adam, Israel, and Jesus that will help us move forward. In the following charts, I've illustrated several significant biblical similarities they share. Each similar characteristic is supported by relevant scripture.

ISRAEL	JESUS	ADAM
SPECIALLY FORMED BY GOD		
"But now, this is what the Lord says – he who created you, Jacob, He who formed you Israel." Isaiah 44:1	"The Word became flesh and dwelt among us." John 1:14	"Then God formed a man from the dust of the ground and breathed into his nostrils the breath of life." Genesis 2:7
CHOSEN BY GOD		
"For the Lord has chosen Jacob to be his own, Israel to be his treasured possession." Psalm 135:4	"He was chosen before the creation of the world." 1 Peter 1:20	"Now the Lord God had planted a garden in the east, in Eden, and there he put the man he had formed." Genesis 2:8
PLACED IN A COVENANT RELATION WITH GOD		
So I will establish my covenant with you, and you will know that I am the Lord." Ezekiel 16: 62	"And a voice from heaven said, "This is my Son whom I love; with him I am well pleased." Matthew 3:17	"As at Adam, they have broken the covenant, they were unfaithful to me there." Hosea 6:7

GIVEN MORAL CHOICES

"See, I am setting before you today a blessing and a curse – the blessing if you obey the commands of the Lord your God that I am giving you today; the curse if you disobey the commands of the Lord your God."

Deuteronomy 11:26

"All this I will give you," he said, "if you will bow down and worship me." Jesus said to him, "Away from me, Satan! For it is written: "Worship the Lord your God, and serve him only."

Mathew 4:9-10

"You are free to eat from any tree in the garden; but you must not eat from the tree of the knowledge of good and evil."

Genesis 2:16

CHOSEN TO DEMONSTRATE GOD TO THE WORLD

"Give praise to the Lord, proclaim his name; make known among the nations what he has done."

1 Chronicles 16:8

"I and the Father are one."

John 10:30

"For as in Adam all die, so in Christ all will be made alive."

1 Corinthians 15:22

NOT THE FIRST

Not the first nation. "Then you will know that I am the Lord your God who brought you out from under the yoke of the Egyptians."

Exodus 6:7

Not the first man. "Thus there were fourteen generations in all from Abraham to David, fourteen from David to the exile in Babylon, and fourteen from the exile to the Messiah."

Matthew 1:17

Not the first Homo sapien. "Let us make mankind."

Genesis 1:26

"Then the Lord formed a man." Genesis 2:7

(also based on anthropological studies)

FIRST OF THEIR KIND

First nation of its kind. "I will take you as my own people, and I will be your God."

Exodus 6:7

First man of his kind. "For in Christ all the fullness of God lives in bodily form."

Colossians 2:9

First Homo sapien of his kind. "Adam, the son of God."

Luke 4:38

As we can see, Israel and Jesus share many special characteristics with Adam and Eve.

The point I really want to emphasize is that Israel was not in any way the first nation on the Earth, nor was Jesus the first man. However, they were both the first of their kind. Not being the very first didn't prevent God from using Israel or his son, Jesus, for very special purposes.

In the same way, it's clear from scripture that Adam and Eve were also formed by God for a special purpose. Based on the pattern seen with Israel and Jesus, we can logically contemplate that Adam and Eve didn't have to be the first Homo sapiens on the Earth to be special.

As we will see in the next chapter, based on the scriptures noted under Adam, there is reason to see that the creation of mankind was an earlier development than the creation of Adam. And yet, like Jesus and Israel, Adam was still the first of his kind to be called the son of God.

This chapter has been meant to provide a context for our discussion about the origins of Adam. My thesis is that Adam was not the first Homo sapiens on the Earth, but he was still the first of his kind. This idea is supported by the examples of Israel and Jesus. It means that we need not presuppose that there was no previous Homo sapiens prior to Adam. In turn, this opens the door to accepting the findings of anthropology, thereby reconciling scripture and science.

The takeaways from this chapter are:

- Israel was specially formed by God for a special purpose but was not the first nation in the world.
- Jesus was also specially formed for a unique purpose but was not the first man.
- Adam was specially formed by God for a special purpose and did not have to be the first Homo sapiens on the Earth for this to be so.
- All three were the first of their kind.

In the next chapter, we will look more closely at how Adam fits in with the rest of humanity.

Twenty-Two

MORE ABOUT ADAM

> When God created mankind, he made them in the
> likeness of God. (Genesis 5:1)

LET'S GO BACK to the precedent established in the week-within-a-week creation model. We saw that the Earth Creation Week was a subset of the Universe Creation Week. In the same way, I am now suggesting that the creative act of forming Adam out of the dust was a subset of the general creation of mankind. I made a case for two different creation accounts: one for the Earth (Genesis 1:2–26) and one for the universe (Genesis 2:1). I also believe there were two different creation events for humanity: one for mankind (Genesis 1:26) and one for Adam (Genesis 2:7).

Let's consider some of the differences found in the two narratives.

GENESIS 1

- Man is given every seed-bearing plant and tree for food.
- Man is told to fill the Earth.
- The name of God is Elohim, which is the general name for God as Creator.
- Man is not given specific moral commandments from God.

GENESIS 2

- Adam is restricted from eating from one tree.
- Adam is placed in a garden.
- The name of God used is Yahweh, or Lord God, which is used in the context of a personal relationship or covenant.
- Adam is given a specific commandment not to eat from the tree of the knowledge of good and evil.

These differences give the impression that these two narratives describe different creation events.

It seems clear that the account in Genesis 2 describes a situation where Adam was specially created with the capacity to make moral choices and enter into a personal relationship with God.

The question is, when did this creation occur? I have already demonstrated that this type of special creation didn't have to occur as the origination of the entire species. Here are some quick facts to establish the timelines involved concerning Homo sapiens according to science:

- The earliest fossils of the genus Homo were found in East Africa and have been dated at 2.3 million years old.[74]
- The oldest recovered DNA of early human relatives comes from the Sima de Los Huesos, the Pit of Bones. These 430,000-year-old remains have been identified as the oldest known Neanderthals.
- Fragments of 300,000-year-old skulls, jaws, and teeth, as well as other fossils found at Jebel Irhoud, are the oldest remains of Homo sapiens yet found.
- Anatomically modern humans dwelt along the Mediterranean some 177,000 to 194,000 years ago.

- We can trace most human ancestry to individuals who were part of a landmark migration out of Africa beginning some fifty thousand to sixty thousand years ago.[75]

The purpose of this brief recap is to outline the findings of anthropological research which establish that hominids preceding and including Homo sapiens, the only surviving species of hominids, have been present on the Earth for a long period of time.

As I did for the creation week, I will clearly define the terms being used for this discussion. In particular, I want to establish a definition for the word "man."

In the Bible, this word is used to describe all people from the time of Adam onward. Psalm 8:4–5 says, *"What is mankind that you are mindful of them, human beings that you care for them? You have made them a little lower than the angels and crowned them with glory and honor."* In Ecclesiastes 3:11 we read, *"He has also set eternity in the human heart."* And Luke 3:38 refers to *"Adam, the son of God."* Thus, the definition of a "man" must recognize that he is made by God and has high spiritual capabilities which provide him unique status and dignity.

In addition, a technical definition of "man" in Webster's Dictionary describes him this way: "a bipedal primate mammal (Homo sapiens) that is anatomically related to the great apes but distinguished especially by notable development of the brain… sole living representative of the hominid family."[76]

The approach this book takes is to accept the findings of modern science. In this context, I agree that early hominids existed. But I believe they didn't have the capacity or opportunity to have a personal covenant relationship with God, something which began with Adam.

Consider two people who share a similar genetic makeup and note that one of them composes classical music while the other is tone-deaf. One person is a famous portrait artist and the other has trouble drawing a stickman.

While not a perfect analogy, this can help us understand that not all members of mankind have the same capabilities or roles.

In describing Adam as the son of God, the Bible implies that there was something inadequate about all the humanity that came before him.

As the American physicist Brian Greene once said, "No matter how hard you try to teach your cat general relativity, you're going to fail."[77] In the same way, I would posit that pre-Adamic mankind was spiritually limited and incapable of a personal spiritual relationship with God. With Adam, God endowed mankind not only with the ability to understand relativity but also the extraordinary capacity to conceive of it all on its own.

Even more critical than the intellectual side, I believe, was the spiritual component that set Adam apart.

Dr. Dennis Bonnette has pointed out, "Since mere matter can never evolve into spirit, true man must have appeared instantly at some point."[78] The Bible seems to confirm this concept of spiritual progression being separate from the physical. We are taught in 1 Corinthians 15:44–46 that if there is a natural body, there is also a spiritual body. So it is written, *"'The first man Adam became a living being'; the last Adam, a life-giving spirit. The spiritual did not come first, but the natural, and after that the spiritual."*

I suggest then that the early Homo sapiens were a form of the natural, which came first. Adam was also spiritual in a special way and created afterwards. In other words, I believe that God started a special program with Adam, who was singular in his capacities and made for a specific role.

My contention is that in the following ways Adam was the first person who:

- Possessed special spiritual capabilities.
- Had the capacity and the opportunity to enter into a perfect covenant relationship with God.
- Was sinless at inception.
- Was born of the Spirit.
- Began the lineage that led to Jesus.

Based on the elements outlined above, I consider Adam to be the first "man."

Some theological parallels can be drawn between pre-Adamic man and the concept of the need to be "born again" found in the gospel. Christ declared,

> Very truly I tell you, no one can see the kingdom of God unless they are born again… Very truly I tell you, no one can enter the kingdom of God unless they are born of water and the Spirit. (John 3:3, 5)

The genetics of Christians who have been born again don't change after conversion. Nevertheless, we see from the above scripture that a spiritual transformation takes place through faith in Christ's redemptive work, instantly qualifying and empowering believers to enter God's kingdom. Thus, being born of the Spirit enables one to have a covenant relationship with God.

However, pre-Adamic man may not have been endowed with the capacity, or have lacked the mechanism or opportunity, to undergo the type of spiritual regeneration required for one to be born of the spirit and fulfill the role Adam did. In contrast, Adam had the spirit breathed into him at inception, at which time he had no sin. So he was able to fulfill the purposes for which he was created, including being the predecessor of Jesus.

As we outlined in the previous chapter, the purposes for which Adam was made compare closely to those pertaining to Israel and Jesus. Also, as a spiritual creation, Adam — and all his descendants — would have qualified to inherit the kingdom of God if Adam had kept his covenant with God. He didn't, so that is why Christ had to be sent as *"the last Adam"* (1 Corinthians 12:45).

Consider this idea in terms of the progressive revelation of God. Paul writes in Romans 5:13,

> To be sure, sin was in the world before the law was given, but sin is not charged against anyone's account where there is no law. Nevertheless, death reigned from the time of Adam to the time of Moses, even over those who did not sin by breaking a command, as did Adam…

Based on this, we can surmise that before Adam there was no specific command from God to obey, no law, and no covenant. Once Adam was created with the unique spiritual capacity to know God and placed in the garden that provided the context of defined choices, he had a new responsibility towards God. That is when the potential for spiritual, covenant-breaking sin arose.

In continuing the progressive revelation, God gave the law to the Israelites, which further increased man's knowledge of and accountability to God. In this way, mankind itself came under the law. But then grace was given to mankind through faith in Christ's redemptive work. And through Christ, the capacity was given to become sons of God. As it says in John 1:12, *"Yet to all who did receive him, to those who believed in his name, he gave the right to become children of God."* The progressive revelation of God to mankind on the Earth was completed.

The last step in the progression is still to come: *"For now we see only a reflection as in a mirror; then we shall see face to face"* (1 Corinthians 13:12).

In summary, I believe that a useful way to understand Adam is to remember Israel. God could not create a nation for himself, for the purposes he had in mind, out of the existing nations and peoples of the world at that time. So he purposely created Israel.

The same was true with Adam. He was therefore the first special man, created by God, through whom God could work his unique purposes.

Let us now return to the question of when Adam came into being. Recall that each day in the Earth Creation Week model is 360 million years long. God's creation of hominids and Homo sapiens occurred on day six—during the latter part of this day, I suggest. The creation of Adam, as a separate event, also occurred on day six, but at the very end of it. In fact, the creation of Adam and Eve was God's last act of creation, and I believe it occurred approximately six thousand years ago.

As an interesting sidenote, and from a developmental standpoint, the existence of pre-Adamic Homo sapiens living concurrently with Adam's descendants appears to have resulted in some interbreeding.

According to Chris Stringer, a professor of palaeobiology, genetic research shows that most people have about two percent Neanderthal DNA.[79]

Philosopher Kenneth W. Kemp proposed that interbreeding between Adam and Eve's descendants and other Homo sapiens could explain the diversity of human genes.[80]

I posit, based on all the finetuning we see in the universe and nature we have touched on in this book, that it is reasonable to conclude that interbreeding created a gene pool ideal for mankind to survive and prosper. Scripture does provide a full record of the lineage from Adam to Jesus, therefore demonstrating that the integrity of this lineage was completely protected regardless of any interbreeding.

From a theological point of view, it is essential that Jesus was directly descended, on the human side, from Adam, who was termed a son of God and born of the Spirit.

Returning to the timeline, I maintain the belief that Adam was created about six or seven thousand years ago based on the genealogies found in the Bible. The genealogies in Genesis are very detailed and structured unambiguously.

This contrasts with other genealogies recorded in the Bible which employ the use of telescoping. Telescoping is a technique where one person is said to beget another, or is the father of another, when the actual lineage may have involved many generations between them. An example of telescoping is found in Matthew 1:8, which references *"Jehoram the father of Uzziah."* However, we know from various passages in 2 Chronicles that Jehoram was the father of Ahazian, who was the father of Joash, who was the father of Amazian, who was the father of Uzziah (2 Chronicles 22:1, 11, 24:27, 26:1). So the original statement is accurate in what it was communicating, but it was abbreviated to leave out several generations.

In contrast, the Genesis genealogy is recorded in a way that precludes telescoping because it records the actual ages of each father and son. For example, Genesis 5:3–6 says,

> When Adam had lived 130 years, he had a son in his own likeness, in his own image; and he named him Seth. After Seth was born, Adam lived 800 years and had other sons and daughters. Altogether, Adam lived a total of 930 years, and then he died. When Seth had lived 105 years, he became the father of Enosh.

Each subsequent generation is recorded in the same way. This means that there are seemingly no unaccounted gaps of time in this genealogy.

That said, some variation is possible, as there are some differences found in the genealogical records of the Masoretic Text version of the Old Testament compared to the Greek Septuagint. We will discuss these differences in detail in Chapter Twenty-Five. Briefly here, the differences could result in Adam having been created approximately seven thousand five hundred years ago compared to about six or seven thousand years ago.

My view is that the motivation to discount the accuracy of the Genesis genealogy has been largely predicated on the incorrect assumption that since Homo sapiens have been in existence for tens or hundreds of thousands of years, then Adam, if he existed at all, must have lived much longer than six thousand years ago.

But I believe that Adam was real and lived relatively recently, in line with the biblical genealogies. I therefore contend that the biblical genealogies are indeed accurate. So Adam wasn't the first Homo sapiens, but he was the first of his kind; he was the first man to have the capacity and opportunity to enter into a covenant relationship with God.

For the interested reader, in Appendix Three I discuss other questions about Adam relating to the Genesis account which are not central to this thesis but still of some value and relevance.

In this chapter, I have relied on scripture to provide a plausible theory for Adam and Eve's special creation approximately six or seven thousand years ago while still affirming the prior existence of other Homo sapiens. This theory therefore doesn't conflict with anthropology. It affirms God as Creator and also fits in with the plausible days theory of the overall model. It also affirms that mankind, including Adam, was created on day six, in agreement with scripture. This thesis meets all the established evaluation criteria.

EVALUATION SCORECARD

✓	✓	✓	✓	✓
SCRIPTURALLY SUPPORTED	AGREES WITH SCIENCE	PLAUSIBLE 'DAYS' OF DEFINED LENGTH	AFFIRMS GOD IS CREATOR	INTERNAL INTEGRITY

Twenty-Three

GOD'S METHODS

> God moves in a mysterious way
> His wonders to perform;
> He plants his footprints in the sea
> and rides upon the storm.[81]
> —William Cowper

IN THIS BOOK, I have offered a completely new framework for understanding the days of Genesis. The timeframes generated by the week-within-a-week creation model align with the natural history of the universe and Earth. This is a pivotal first step in harmonizing science and scripture because it removes a long-standing and central obstacle to the acceptance of the Bible as a credible source of information.

The purpose of this book is to demonstrate how science and scripture can be fully reconciled in a plausible manner. Its purpose is not to prove God; this cannot be done. Nor is its purpose to prove anything false. This is the reason I use the word *plausible*. If I can construct a theory that plausibly accommodates all verified information available from every area of study, that will be sufficient to allow the possibility for God to be God and the Bible to be true without strong objections raised.

The long timeframes of creation which this model supports are also consistent with the processes of evolution. Evolution is a process of biological change and development caused by genetic mutation and driven by natural selection as organisms survive or die in changing environments over massive amounts of time, and its existence is well-documented and established by science. The gene pool of surviving organisms continues and thus contains the inventory of genetic information on which future changes depend. This book acknowledges that evolution has occurred.

At this point, I wish to briefly address the seeming dichotomy between the biblical process of lifeforms reproducing exclusively after their kind (Genesis 1:11, 21, 24) and the broad and continuous changes presented by evolution. I posit that both processes are true, based on current evidence—that is, we know that animals and plants reproduce within their own species. In that sense, the Bible is completely accurate.

But even today, subtle and gradual changes have been observed in the same species. For example, new traits have been recorded in central European blackcap birds, precipitated by changes in migration and mating patterns that occurred over a fifty-year period.[82] Thus, both processes are seen to be at work in the natural world and can be surmised to have always been at work, but on different timescales.

Turning back to my goal of proposing a plausible reconciliation between the processes of evolution and special creation, I pose this question: can the theory of evolution accommodate all testimony from scripture?

Starting in Genesis 2:7 we read, *"Then the Lord God formed a man from the dust of the ground and breathed into his nostrils the breath of life, and the man became a living being."* In this passage, we can see that Adam's creation is not consistent with the processes that drive evolution.

In Psalm 148:2–5 we find,

> Praise him, all his angels; praise him, all his heavenly hosts. Praise him, sun and moon; praise him, all you shining stars. Praise him, you highest heavens and you waters above the skies. Let them praise the name of the Lord, for at his command they were created…

This passage is very instructive, as angels are included in the list of created things. Angels, as described in the scriptures, are celestial beings similar to mankind in some respects but holy and more powerful.

Psalm 8:4–5 says, *"What is mankind that you are mindful of them, human beings that you care for them? You have made them a little lower than the angels and crowned them with glory and honor."*

Angels came into existence through God's command, but it is also clear that evolutionary processes were not involved. Angels don't procreate, nor do they die, so there is no mechanism for the evolution of angels to occur.

As we are told in Matthew 22:30, *"At the resurrection people will neither marry nor be given in marriage; they will be like the angels in heaven."* This passage establishes God's ability to create beings outside of evolution, as well as the precedent that he has indeed done so.

The goal here is to point out that while God has used evolutionary processes in nature, it would seem clear from scripture that God's creative processes are not limited by them. It is therefore reasonable to ask: if God, through his power, specially created angels who are greater than men, what would prevent him from creating a man such as Adam in a similar manner?

Based on the above discussion, the answer to whether evolution can fully accommodate scripture is clearly no. Many statements in scripture cannot be explained by or are inconsistent with evolution, such as the creation of Adam, the raising of Lazarus (John 11:1–4), and the incarnation and resurrection of Christ, to name but a few.

Now let's turn this question around: can scripture fully accommodate evolution? To answer, let's look at the scriptures and review some examples of God's relationship with the natural world.

We can start by looking at the Earth's hydrological cycle, whereby water evaporates from the oceans and lakes of the world and condenses into clouds. Eventually, the moisture in clouds becomes too heavy and results in precipitation, replenishing river systems and providing sustenance to all terrestrial life. And then, in an endless cycle, the water flows back to the sea.

This process was described many times in scripture before it was understood scientifically. Job 36:27–28 says, *"He draws up the drops of water, which distill as rain to the streams; the clouds pour down their moisture and abundant showers fall on mankind."* Then in Ecclesiastes 1:7 we read, *"All streams flow into the sea, yet the sea is never full. To the place the streams come from, there they return again."*

We better understand the natural mechanisms which drive this cycle than people did in biblical history. From looking at the processes of evaporation and condensation, we observe, because of the heat of the sun and other ambient conditions which cause water to vaporize, that there is no need to ascribe any personal intervention by God to explain this ongoing process. Rather, the process is mechanical, independent, and sustainable on its own.

Yet perplexingly the scriptures still maintain that God somehow remains personally and intimately involved in this natural process, as well as all others. For example, Jeremiah 14:22 gives direct credit to God:

> Do any of the worthless idols of the nations bring
> rain? Do the skies themselves send down showers?
> No, it is you, Lord our God. Therefore our hope is in
> you, for you are the one who does all this.

I believe there are a few key takeaways from this example in nature:

- The Bible correctly identified the elements of the hydrological cycle prior to any scientific understanding of it.
- God is involved in this cycle by creating the conditions which make the system work: heat from the sun, the geography of the Earth—with mountains and hills, above which water is cooled and condensed into rainclouds—and the elevation differentiation that allows for water to flow toward the sea. There are also deeper considerations, such as the properties of water itself, the specific gravity of which changes with its temperature. Also, if the Earth was farther from the sun, all water would freeze and never evaporate. Conversely, if the Earth was closer, water vapour would never condense into rain. Thus, many components need to be finely tuned.
- Notwithstanding that this system is independent and sustainable based on the nature of the Earth, God is described as being intimately involved in all that occurs and, ultimately, in control. For example, God specifically prevented rain from falling for three and a half years in response to Elijah's prayer (James 5:17). Another time, God caused a purposeful deluge of rain for forty days and forty nights (Genesis 7:8).
- The systems and laws which God has ordained do not preclude him from working through them or outside them.

Before moving on, it's important to appreciate the qualities and characteristics of God revealed by the hydrological cycle. The cycles associated with God all support life. Isaiah 30:23 says,

> He will also send you rain for the seed you sow in the ground, and the food that comes from the land will be rich and plentiful. In that day your cattle will graze in broad meadows.

This and many other scriptures associate the falling of rain and flowing of water with a renewal of the land. Also of note is how this cycle mirrors the purposes of God. In Isaiah 55:10–11 we are told,

> As the rain and the snow come down from heaven, and do not return to it without watering the earth and making it bud and flourish, so that it yields seed for the sower and bread for the eater, so is my word that goes out from my mouth: It will not return to me empty, but will accomplish what I desire…

The beneficial and effective nature of the hydrological cycle is compared to the benefits and effectiveness of all that God says and does.

In contrast to this, many cycles in human life are not life-affirming. For example, domestic abuse often repeats from generation to generation. Or consider the cycle of physical inactivity whereby the body becomes weaker and more susceptible to injury. As a result, a person can lose confidence and avoid exercise, thus reinforcing the cycle. Eventually, and in the extreme, such a cycle will lead to death.

Certainly, neither of these cycles is healthy or life-affirming. The point I'm trying to make is that God's cycles are always consistent with his character.

Lastly, let's consider all the beauty associated with the hydrological cycle. Everything about it—the clouds in the sky, a soft summer rain, the rainbow, the flowing brook, flourishing flowers and fauna—results in wondrous beauty. In that sense, we see the character of God revealed in what could otherwise be categorized only as an impersonal and mechanical system, driven by cold physics. His character is revealed by the outcomes produced.

Matthew 7:16 tells us, *"By their fruit you will recognize them."* Thus we arrive at these familiar lyrics: "All things bright and beautiful, all creatures great and small, all things wise and wonderful, the Lord God made them all."[83]

The takeaways from this review of scripture are that God:

- Uses natural cycles and processes to accomplish his plans.
- Sometimes acts outside of nature.
- Creates cycles which are life-affirming.
- Uses nature to reveal his character.
- Reveals his purposes, love, and wisdom through these processes.

The beauty and wonder of nature suggest a spiritual component as opposed to being merely mechanical and barren of meaning. As Albert Einstein said, "There are only two ways to live your life. One is as though nothing is a miracle. The other is as though everything is a miracle."[84]

Something else to consider is that God is described in scripture as being intimately involved in creation. For example, Psalm 139:13–14 says, *"For you created my inmost being; you knit me together in my mother's womb. I praise you because I am fearfully and wonderfully made; your works are wonderful, I know that full well."* This is another paradox: God uses natural embryological processes to create new life over a span of time, as in the case of evolution, while remaining involved and responsible for the miracle of it all.

This is all to say that God's relationship with his creation is not simplistic or one-dimensional. He is outside of his perfectly planned creation, which operates based on the laws he created. But he is also omnipresent, omniscient, omnipotent, and intimately and always involved in everything. In this sense, he is all in all and Lord of all.

In light of these considerations, let's return to the discussion of evolution. Like the hydrological cycle, evolution can be seen as a mechanism through which God achieves his purposes.

Evolutionary processes have facilitated the adaptive diversification and survival of plants and animals over millions of years. The timeframes of the week-within-a-week creation model and modern scientific data can be aligned, so there is no conflict between scripture and the process or timing of any evolutionary developments other than those passages where the Bible specifically states that God acted outside of this mechanism. This is not unlike those times when he acted outside the natural hydrological cycle, using it supernaturally.

In the case of evolution and the immense amount of time needed for it, the picture is one of continuous, undirected, and random change. This seems to be a much different process than that of instantaneous, special creation. But I would suggest that these two concepts aren't necessarily mutually exclusive.

To help unravel this apparent dichotomy, we can perhaps consider the march of time as it relates to human birth and death.

For example, the physical process of embryological development is gradual, each stage being well-documented and expected. But when the child arrives, we still ask ourselves, "Where did this precious and unique soul suddenly come from?" Thus, the development of a baby can be characterized as both slow and expected and sudden and miraculous.

Similarly, the birth and death of a generation of mankind is gradual and to be expected as a natural consequence of the passage of time. But when many people in one generation eventually die, it is common to refer to the situation as the end of an era. Thus, a sudden division of time is employed to highlight subjectively important changes, as gradual as they may have been.

In the same way, I contend that the slow and gradual processes of evolution do not preclude sudden changes or special creations by God. And we shouldn't expect these special creative acts by God to be of a simplistic, fairy-tale nature. Rather, they are wonderfully diverse, complex, and marvellous. Just like Christ walking upon the water, such things are beyond us.

In fact, the incarnation of God in Christ is an example of special formation. The advent of Christ approached slowly through history, winding through generations of his natural ancestral line. However, it also came suddenly, through a divine act of God.

And Christ's life and death resulted in the most profound division of time in history.

I believe then that this analogy contains some important parallels with the methods God used in the creation of our world: they are both long, drawn-out processes over time and also sudden and special creative acts.

In summary, I think it's never wise to underestimate either God's power or the truth contained in the Genesis account of creation.

In my view, the greatest understanding of the appearance of life throughout time is this: all the incredible instincts and adaptations seen in animals; the innumerable shapes, colours, and capabilities evident in both flora and fauna; and everything inexplicable, beautiful, and amazing found in the natural world first came into being in the infinite and wondrous imagination of God. I believe that nothing has appeared that he did not know about or plan. How he chose to bring these things into physical reality, and how long he took to do so, is of secondary importance. But I am confident that all the different ways he brought his creation into being were purposeful and amazing.

It is not possible to know all that God has done or how he has done it—that is, other than what scripture and science tell us.

Even science cannot tell us everything. For example, science cannot categorically identify where the energy needed for the origin of our universe came from, nor how the laws that govern the universe came to be. Science hasn't been able to replicate the creation of life. There are also aspects of the spontaneous appearance of complex lifeforms which still pose problems.

Based on these unknowns, I suggest that it is reasonable to embrace the biblical claim that God is the Creator, as this position cannot be refuted or categorically proven wrong by science. In other words, my position is that while scripture cannot be accommodated by evolution, evolution can indeed fit into a sound scriptural interpretation. In this way, a plausible harmony between science and Genesis can be achieved.

I believe the week-within-a-week creation model provides a transformative explanation of the days of the Genesis narrative and a timeline that doesn't conflict with evolutionary science. I also believe God still used special creation at times in the manner of his choosing. Thus, my conviction is that regardless of what processes God used, he was still behind it all.

In the next chapter, we will examine this claim in more detail.

Twenty-Four

THE MIRACLE OF LIFE

> Poems are made by fools like me, but only God can
> make a tree.[85] — Joyce Kilmer

IN THE LAST chapter, we looked at God's methods and how, through faith, God's character can be perceived in the wonderful things that have been created, regardless of how and when that happened.

Something else to consider is the sheer complexity of life and all the inexplicable features found in nature.

The purpose of this chapter is not to evaluate evolutionary science, as that would be beyond the scope of this book and the expertise of the author. Rather, it is to provide a few examples of amazing complexity that have been discovered in nature, with the view to increase our appreciation of the world we live in and help us reflect on the part God played in it all.

I also look to show how this subject directly ties in with the overall thesis of this book.

An example of biological complexity can be observed in bacterial flagella. A flagellum is a hair-like protrusion on a bacterium which provides it with mobility. The flagellum is like a propeller on a motorboat and is attached to an axle that extends through a bearing of sorts and is driven by a biological motor within the bacterium. The fastest flagellum was recorded by laser microscopy to spin at a rate of 100,000 rotations per minute. The system has three different components consisting of forty different proteins. All its parts need to be in place for the flagellum to work and its assembly is completed spontaneously. The parts for the flagellum need to be manufactured in a microscopic factory, so to speak, in a precise and inflexible order and then transported to where the system is constructed. All this is done at a microscopic level, requiring magnification of fifty thousand times to render it observable.[86]

The programming needed to create such a marvel of engineering is contained and directed by DNA in the form of an extremely complex code, or blueprint, for the organism. It appears to be impossible for the proteins, which are folded and attached to one another to form organisms, to assemble themselves without the DNA code. And how would the DNA form itself independently of the organisms that contain it?

These questions highlight the complexity found in nature and all the questions and wonder it stimulates.

Regarding DNA, I turn to Dr. Doug Corrigan, who holds a PhD in biochemistry and molecular biology. He explains:

> The 6 billion bits of information that comprise the DNA in our cells is approximately 6 feet long. This 6 feet of DNA in each of our cells is folded up and compacted into a microscopically-sized nucleus. If all of the DNA in our entire body was unwound and connected end-to-end, it would stretch 34 billion miles, or 1.4 million times around the earth!
>
> ...This folding pattern [of the DNA] allows the nucleus of each cell to possess an information density that is trillions of times higher than modern microchips.[87]

Corrigan thus provides more detail as to the extraordinary level of complexity and amazing qualities found throughout nature and life, even at the molecular level.

Nicholas Wade, a science writer for *The New York Times*, wrote:

> No one has yet devised a plausible explanation to show how the earliest chemicals of life—thought to be RNA, or ribonucleic acid, a close relative of DNA—might have constructed themselves from the inorganic chemicals likely to have been around on the early earth. The spontaneous assembly of small RNA molecules on the primitive earth "would have been a near miracle."[88]

Even with all available technology, man cannot begin to replicate cell structure, let alone bring a cell to life. W.H. Thorpe, an evolutionist scientist, has acknowledged, "The most elementary type of cell constitutes a 'mechanism' unimaginably more complex that any machine yet thought up, let alone constructed by man."[89]

A cell is made up of thousands of complex protein molecules. Proteins are molecules consisting of smaller units called amino acids arranged in a specific sequence. Unless the exact sequence is followed, the protein becomes useless. Therefore, the probability of an average-sized protein molecule forming on its own in a useful way has been calculated to be one in 10^{300}. And that's just one protein molecule. In a single bacterium, there are two thousand types of proteins![90]

But there are even more complexities to be considered. DNA can only replicate with the help of special proteins called enzymes. However, the synthesis of proteins depends on the information within the DNA, meaning that both must exist at the same time.

American microbiologist Homer Jacobsen has commented on this problem:

> Directions for the reproduction of plans, for energy and the extraction of parts from the current environment, for the growth sequence, and for the effector mechanism translating instructions into growth, all had to be simultaneously present at that moment (when life began). This combination of events has seemed an incredibly unlikely happenstance, and has often been ascribed to divine intervention.[91]

James Tour, a professor of chemistry, computer science, materials science, and nanoengineering at Rice University, has more than 680 research publications to his name. He said,

> We have no idea how the basic set of molecules, carbohydrates, nucleic acids, lipids and proteins, were made and how they could have coupled in proper sequences, and then transformed into the ordered assemblies until there was the construction of a complex biological system, and eventually to that first cell. Nobody has any idea on how this was done when using our commonly understood mechanisms of chemical science. Those that say that they understand are generally wholly uninformed regarding chemical synthesis![92]

And regarding the origin of life, British mathematician and astronomer Fred Hoyle once commented,

> Life cannot have a random beginning... the trou-
> ble is that there are about 2000 enzymes, and the
> chance of obtaining them all in a random trial is only
> one part in 10 to the 40,000 power, an outrageously
> small probability that could not be faced even if the
> whole universe consisted of organic soup.[93]

So from the smallest cell to the one thousand billion trillion stars in space, everything studied by scientists is unfathomably complex.[94]

And in addition to the mystery of the origins of life, other questions remain unanswered, such as:

- The beginning of the universe.
- How complex systems could arise spontaneously.
- The source of the laws governing the universe.
- The sudden origin of body plans in the Cambrian explosion.[95]

The origins of the laws of physics and mathematics that govern the universe also present a quandary.

As just one example of universal mathematical relationships, we can consider the fine-structure constant. The fine-structure constant is a measure of the strength of the interaction between charged particles and the electromagnetic force.[96]

This constant is dimensionless, independent of the system used, and has a value of 1/137.035999084. It has many applications in physics. Based on the anthropic principle, the fine-structure constant has the value it does because if it were any different, life and intelligent beings could not exist.[97] If this force were less powerful, no electrons would stay in orbit around the nucleus of atoms. If it was more powerful, electrons would not bond with other atoms, meaning that no atoms could exist.

Max Born, awarded the Nobel Prize in Physics for research in quantum mechanics, said, "It is clear that the explanation of this number must be the central problem of natural philosophy."[98]

Richard Feynman, one of the developers of quantum electrodynamics, said this about the fine-structure constant:

> Immediately you would like to know where this number for a coupling comes from: is it related to [pi] or perhaps to the base of natural logarithms? Nobody knows. It's one of the greatest damn mysteries of physics: a magic number that comes to us with no understanding by man. You might say the "hand of God" wrote that number, and "we don't know how He pushed his pencil."[99]

In addition to this number, there are other constants found in nature:

THE GRAVITATIONAL CONSTANT

- If this force was greater, stars would burn too fast and would burn out before life could arise.
- If it was less, stars could not start their thermonuclear fusion.[100]

STRONG FORCE COUPLING CONSTANT

- If weaker, atoms would not hold together.
- If stronger, all elements lighter than iron would be rare.
- Radioactive decay rates would be less which would affect reduce the heating of the Earth.[101]

Earlier, we spoke about the Hubble constant. It's interesting to note that if the Hubble constant was only a bit slower, the universe would have imploded back on itself before stars could have formed. And if it were much higher, stars and galaxies could not have coalesced.[102]

So we see again that the building blocks of the universe and life are found to be finetuned in the only way that makes life possible. We also find that nature functions according to a coherent set of physical laws.

As Einstein remarked, "One may say the eternal mystery of the world is its comprehensibility."[103]

There are endless examples of amazingly complex systems seen in nature that boggle the mind. But by touching on the fine-structure constant and the five hundred types of finetuning of the universe, it becomes clear that a myriad of conditions must be in place for life, and for us, to exist.

In other words, scientists have found that things are the way they are because that's the only way we could exist. It's the only way we could be here to examine and study the universe. Since there is intelligent life on the Earth, the anthropic principle holds that either the universe was designed for this purpose or it was in some way a fluke.[104]

From the examples noted, we find evidence in science that the universe is designed and operates in a way that supports life as we know it. At the same time, when we look at the Genesis narrative, we see that God created all things in a way that would support life so he could have a relationship with man.

Thus, we have further confirmation of my thesis: reconciliation of science and scripture is possible even at the existential level. A logical extension of this thinking would be that the extent to which God used time, evolutionary processes, and special creation is predicated upon that special combination of factors which allows for things to work as they do.

As Thomas Edison once remarked, "Until man duplicates a blade of grass, nature can laugh at his so-called scientific knowledge."[105] To such remarks, evolutionists might reply that the incredible phenomena found in nature neither prove that a belief in God is right nor prove evolution is wrong.

But I would submit that this is not the real point. The point is that everything in the universe and nature is observed to work toward the purposes of life. And as long as life endures, the vast wonders of nature will continue to cause heads to bow and hearts to ponder.

Twenty-Five

THE FLOOD AND NOAH'S ARK

> To doubt everything or to believe everything are two equally convenient solutions; both dispense with the necessity of reflection.[106] —Jules Henri Poincare

THE BIBLICAL FLOOD story is important and well-known, but it's often dismissed as fanciful and false. It's widely assessed to be a synthesis of ancient mythologies, not to be taken literally.

Because of profound misunderstandings and deep scepticism surrounding this narrative, many people have consequently rejected the Bible as a whole. For this reason, I believe it's important to review the flood narrative, as I've done with the creation story, and evaluate it to see whether it can be rationally understood in a literal manner.

This is not to say that the Genesis flood narrative can be definitively proven. Rather, I propose that there is a credible basis for believing it, just as I believe in the days of creation and Adam and Eve.

Let me begin by reviewing some reasons why the flood narrative should be considered true. First, it's an indispensable part of the biblical testimony. Christ himself directly referred to Noah's flood:

> Just as it was in the days of Noah, so also will it be in the days of the Son of Man. People were eating,

drinking, marrying and being given in marriage up to the day Noah entered the ark. Then the flood came and destroyed them all… It will be just like this on the day the Son of Man is revealed. (Luke 17:26–27, 30)

In 2 Peter 2:5 we read that *"he did not spare the ancient world when he brought the flood on its ungodly people, but protected Noah, a preacher of righteousness, and seven others."*

Paul wrote in Hebrews 11:7, *"By faith Noah, when warned about things not yet seen, in holy fear built an ark to save his family."*

We also read,

But they deliberately forget that long ago by God's word the heavens came into being and the earth was formed out of water and by water. By these waters also the world of that time was deluged and destroyed. By the same word the present heavens and earth are reserved for fire, being kept for the day of judgment and destruction of the ungodly. (2 Peter 3:5–7)

All in all, Noah is mentioned fifty-one times in the Bible. In addition to Genesis, there are references to him in eight other books.[107]

Further, mankind was repopulated from the remnant of Noah, and these people subsequently built the tower of Babel. From there, people were divided and dispersed, some of whom were destroyed at Sodom and Gomorrah. Noah was the direct ancestor of Abraham, Jacob, Moses, King David, and Jesus.

In the verses referenced above, we are told that God's word (Jesus) created all things and then destroyed the ancient world. We are also told that he will ultimately destroy the existing heavens by fire and judge mankind.

Thus, the scope of God's plan, including the creation, judgment, and salvation of mankind, is inextricably integrated with Noah's flood. It would therefore seem difficult, if not impossible, to understand the Bible if Noah's flood had not occurred.

The second reason for believing the flood account is that it's clearly presented as an accurate and authoritative record. The Bible provides so many specific details. For example, Genesis 7:11 reports, *"In the six hundredth year of Noah's life, on the seventeenth day of the second month—on that day all the springs of the great deep burst forth, and the floodgates of the heavens were opened."* Then Genesis 8:13 specifically says, *"By the first day of the first month of Noah's six hundred and first year, the water had dried up from the earth."*

It is difficult to conceive why so many specific details would be presented if it wasn't done in good faith.

A third reason to consider the flood account credible is that it's one of many flood legends found in ancient documents. For example, the Epic of Gilgamesh was written in cuneiform on clay tablets and recorded around 2000 BC. It records many details of a flood which are remarkably similar to the Genesis account. For example, both manuscripts indicate:

1. A flood occurred in response to God's (or the gods') displeasure with mankind.
2. A flood resulted in the death of the world.
3. A man, either Noah or Utnapishtim, was given the divine order to build a boat.
4. The boat was to be covered in pitch, be several stories high, and have one door.
5. Family members were to be brought along as passengers.
6. While on the water, they were to send out a bird, a raven or dove, to find land.
7. They were to make a sacrifice to God after the voyage.[108]

This list isn't exhaustive, but the many similarities suggest that the two accounts are based on a collective memory of actual events.

Another confirmation of the flood event comes from the list of Sumerian kings. There are several existing versions of this list. The best known is the Weld-Blundell Prism, which is preserved in cuneiform text on a rectangular clay structure. It records eight antediluvian god-kings who reigned from several different cities in Sumeria before the flood.

The list claims that, after a number of antediluvian rulers, the flood "swept over everything." Afterward, the "kingship once again descended from heaven." Then the list of dynasties and rulers continues.[109]

The Sumerian king list has long been an enigma, as it ascribes thousands of years to the reigns of many kings. Although the subject lies beyond the scope of this chapter, researchers have shown that the thousands of years mentioned are actually a record of days; reasonable timeframes can be understood.[110]

What is important to note is that this independent record attests to a flood that separates the history of the civilization and specifically divides the time between rulers.

The Epic of Atrahasis also provides a detailed account of a great flood, the protagonist of which is Atrahasis, a Noah-like figure. It is preserved on three tablets written in Babylonian and Assyrian and is dated from around 1600 BC. It speaks about the construction of the ark, the boarding of the ark, the great deluge, and the anger of the gods against men.[111]

Another important artifact is a cuneiform clay tablet called the Ark Tablet, dated from 1700 BC. It records the animals proceeding two by two into the ark. It also provides instructions for building the ark, which is described as being round. The tablet describes the material and measurements used to build it, including palm-fibre rope, wooden ribs, and hot bitumen to waterproof the craft. It describes the ark's specific dimensions.[112]

Details like these reinforce the argument that something real and specific occurred.

In addition to these records, cultures around the world have hundreds of flood stories. These legends often share common themes and suggest a shared experience.

This does not mean, however, that the Genesis narrative was derived solely from Babylonian sources, as some have suggested. Scholar John D. Currid writes,

> The uniqueness of the biblical account is a good argument for its independence from rather than its dependence on the pagan mythic texts. They are perhaps two separate traditions that stem from a historical flood. I have written elsewhere, "If the biblical stories are true, one would not be surprised to see those truths in extra-biblical literature. And indeed in ancient Near Eastern myth we do see some kernels of historical truth."[113]

Based on these reasons, there is a basis for believing that the flood narratives relate to a real and important historical event.

For those who believe the biblical flood was real, there are two main theories. One is that the flood was global in scope and the waters covered the entire planet. The other view is that the flood, while very large, was regional.

Many scientific explanations demonstrate that a global flood did not and could not have occurred. For the interested reader, I provide a summary of these arguments in Appendix Four. The purpose of this book is to provide a plausible alignment of scripture with scientific evidence and facts. Accordingly, based on the many reasons listed in the appendix, a global flood does not meet my evaluation criteria of agreeing with science. Therefore, the concept of a global flood must be rejected.

A REGIONAL FLOOD

Going forward, I will focus on the second theory, one that supports the idea of a very large flood in the Mesopotamian floodplain that is now Iraq and the Persian Gulf. I will present the geologic evidence that supports this case. I also hope to explain how a faithful and reasonable reading of scripture can support a local flood understanding.

To start, let's look at Genesis 7:18–19, which has led many people over the years to interpret that the flood was global:

> The waters rose and increased greatly on the earth,
> and the ark floated on the surface of the water. They
> rose greatly on the earth, and all the high mountains
> under the entire heavens were covered.

The inference taken here is that *"all the high mountains"* include Mount Everest, for example. However, the Hebrew word used in this passage is *har*. According to the Hebrew Lexicon, the definition of *har* is a hill, mountain, hill country, or mount, and it is used in diverse ways throughout the Bible.[114]

A plausible and reasonable understanding of this verse is that the waters rose above the highest hills in the expansive flood area.

In Genesis 7:20, this idea is validated by measurements taken to determine the depth of the water where the ark floated. The minimum depth measured by Noah was fifteen cubits (approximately twenty-three feet). Such a depth would be consistent with the concept of a local flood but wouldn't make sense for a global flood for a number of reasons.

First, Noah's voyage started and ended in the Mesopotamian floodplain, so that's presumably the vicinity where any depth measurement would have been taken. If the flood had extended globally, the depth of the water in Mesopotamia where Noah was located would have been more than twenty-nine thousand feet deep. This alone means that the most reasonable understanding is that the flood was large but localized.

In Genesis 7:23 we read, *"Every living thing on the face of the earth was wiped out; people and animals and the creatures that move along the ground and the birds were wiped from the earth."* On first reading, this passage could also be taken to mean that the flood was global in scope.

However, the Hebrew words *kol erets* are used here, which are best translated as "whole earth" or "all land." In the Old Testament, this is nearly always used to describe a local area of land rather than the entire planet.[115] For example, Genesis 2:13 says, *"The name of the second river is Gihon; it winds through the entire* [kol] *land* [erets] *of Cush."* So the term used likely does not reference a global reality but rather something limited to a certain country.

Kol erets is also used in the Bible to speak about mankind. Here are just two of many examples of this.

Genesis 41:57 reports, *"And all the world came to Egypt to buy grain from Joseph, because the famine was severe everywhere."* No one would conclude that this meant people came from South America, for example, to buy food.

A second example is found in 2 Chronicles 9:28: *"Solomon's horses were imported from Egypt and from all other countries."* These terms are again used to describe a widespread area.

In the same way, the Hebrew term *kol erets* is used to describe a local but massive flood.

The Mesopotamian floodplain lies in the area of modern-day Iraq, which extends 1,600 kilometres from the Persian Gulf to Syria and Turkey and one thousand kilometres from Iran to Saudi Arabia, covering 1.6 million square kilometres. The low-lying Mesopotamian delta surrounding the Tigris and Euphrates rivers covers 140,000 square miles.[116]

This vast area encompassed the entire ancient world and is known as the cradle of civilization.[117] For Noah, the flood covered all the land in his known world and killed everything in it.

I believe it is helpful to understand and interpret scripture through Noah's perspective in this way. For example, based on the height of the ark provided by the Bible, and taking into account the curvature of the Earth, a reasonable calculation can be made as to how far Noah would have been able to see. That distance is about fifteen kilometres to the horizon in all directions, representing an area of approximately seven hundred square kilometres.[118]

This line of sight would have made sense in a flood area of potentially tens of thousands of square kilometres or more. For Noah and the people of his time, as far as the eye could see they were surrounded by water and water only. This accounts for Genesis 6:19, which says that *"all the high mountains under the entire heavens were covered."*

Another important internal validation of this concept is found in Genesis 8:5, which speaks of the time after the rain had stopped: *"The waters continued to recede until the tenth month, and on the first day of the tenth month the tops of the mountains became visible."* Forty days later, they sent out a dove: *"But the dove could find nowhere to perch because there was water over all the surface of the earth…"* (Genesis 8:9) At this time, the mountaintops had already been exposed for forty days, but the term *kol erets* is still used to describe water cover the Earth. If mountains could be seen, the waters didn't literally cover the Earth. This demonstrates that scripture uses the term "whole earth" in a hyperbolic but still accurate manner. Thus far, I have tried to show that a localized flood can be supported by scripture. I will now look at the geology and climate conditions in Mesopotamia, and beyond, to determine how Noah's flood could have occurred. Despite the challenges, I will present plausible estimates of the flood's placement in history.

GEOLOGY OF MESOPOTAMIA FLOODPLAIN

It is interesting that the biblical flood began in the Mesopotamian delta, where Noah lived. The geography of this area lends itself to the possibility of a large, sudden flood in the manner described in the Bible. In my view, this susceptible geographic context also adds credibility to the narrative.

Regarding the topography of this area, Steve Sarigasnis wrote,

> The Mesopotamian region forms a huge U-shaped bowl that stretches 600 miles from the Persian Gulf to the northwest. Steep escarpments that rise quickly from less than 200 meters to 1,000 meters set boundaries for the Mesopotamian Plain on the north and the east. Terrain that rises gradually, but consistently, to heights above 400 meters forms the southern and western boundaries. Elevations above 400 meters fully contain the Mesopotamian Plain except where it meets the sea.[119]

The Bible makes it evident that Noah's flood was unlike any other that had occurred in that region by orders of magnitude. Its intensity and destructive impact on life were unmatched. I hope to demonstrate that it was, in fact, the perfect storm.

This perfect storm scenario is described by geologist Jeffery Rose:

> The Gulf Oasis is consistent with the biblical account of Noah's flood. A long torrential rain storm, a tectonic event bursting forth water from

subterranean aquifers, water from the Indian Ocean rushing through the Strait of Hormuz, plus a heat wave generating a sudden melt of snow in the surrounding mountains would have caused a devastating flood wiping out all inhabitants in the Gulf Oasis, the Mesopotamian Plain, and many of the regions surrounding Mesopotamia and what is now the Persian Gulf. Such an event would be perfectly consistent with everything Genesis 6–9 says about Noah's flood.[120]

If the vast majority of the human population lived on the Mesopotamian plain at the time of a major flood, it would have destroyed civilization in that region. This geographical area could have included present-day Iraq, Iran, Kuwait, Saudi Arabia, and Syria, a very important area indeed.

Another geologic feature of Noah's flood relates to the fountains of the deep described in Genesis 7:11. We are told, *"In the six hundredth year of Noah's life, on the seventeenth day of the second month—on that day all the springs of the great deep burst forth, and the floodgates of the heavens were opened."*

So what were the springs of the great deep? The Zagros Mountains in Iran, east of Mesopotamia, are often covered with winter snow and experience large amounts of rainfall during storms. When this snow melts, or when large amounts of rain are produced, some of this water is carried away in surface drainage. However, much of it soaks into the ground, into fractures in bedrock, to eventually move through tunnels in limestone and emerge as springs that feed the Tigris.

A rapid melting of a large amount of mountain snow could have completely saturated the tunnels and groundwater prior to the flood. At the onset of the deluge of rain, these fountains of the deep burst forth. Further to this, Collins notes,

This spring water and surface water in streams flowing from the Zagros Mountains would then flow down the Tigris River and produce perhaps half of the volume of Noah's Flood.[121]

Once the deluge was over and the rains ceased, we are told in Genesis 8:1 that God removed the floodwaters by sending a wind. Why, one might ask, is this fact specifically referenced? Again, it relates to the geology of the area. After the flood crested, the rate at which the waters would have flowed out to the Persian Gulf had to be dependent on the slope of the land. From four hundred miles northwest of Ur on the Persian Gulf, the Euphrates and Tigris rivers drop just three hundred feet in elevation.

This drop provides a grade of only about 0.01 percent. With such a gentle slope, the floodwaters would have moved very slowly. Moreover, for several months after the rain stopped, any water that exited to the gulf would have been replaced with runoff from springs and melting snow on the distant mountains that surround the Mesopotamian plain.[122]

Such a scenario is consistent with the worst floods that have struck the Mississippi Valley, for example. In one case, the water rose fifty feet above the banks but then seemed to remain almost stationary without discernible movement. It was months before the water dried up.[123]

Can evaporation be effective in removing flood waters? Steve Sariganis explains:

During a typical Southern California summer the swimming pools lose an average of one inch of water per day to evaporation. Lower humidity, higher heat, and a strong wind can triple or quadruple that rate. Over the 335 days during which Noah's

Flood receded, that would add up to 84–112 feet of evaporation. If gravity had removed about half that much water, the total water depth removed would have been 126-168 feet.[124]

That is easily enough water to account for Noah's seeing nothing but water for as far as his eyes could see. That is also easily enough water to destroy all of Noah's contemporaries and their animals outside the ark, not to mention enough water to carry the ark to the foothills of Ararat.

THE VIABILITY OF THE ARK

The shape of the ark has conventionally been depicted as a long, rectangular barge, based on the dimensions provided in Genesis: three hundred cubits long, fifty cubits wide, and thirty cubits high. A cubit is roughly the distance from the inside of the elbow to the tip of the middle finger, or between eighteen and twenty-one inches. Different metal cubit measuring rods have been found to be 20.55 inches and 20.8 inches in length.[125]

Based on the cubit measurements provided, the ark could have been 450 to 515 feet long. Such a size would represent the largest wooden vessel ever constructed by man. The *Wyoming* schooner, completed in 1919, had a deck of 350 feet, by comparison.[126]

Being made of wood, the *Wyoming* flexed and twisted in heavy seas and allowed water to intrude. It required metal braces to provide structural support. The ship required pumps to discharge the water taken on and eventually sank in heavy seas five years after its christening.

The dimensions of the ark were said to have been even larger than the Wyoming, and it was built four to five thousand years ago with limited technology. For this reason, many experts believe that an ancient wooden ark of such enormous size could never even have been built, let alone survived a tumultuous, year-long flood.[127]

The huge size of the ark has been met with deep scepticism over the years. It doesn't seem realistic or possible to many people. In addressing this concern, I am going to advance an explanation that is intriguing, counterintuitive, and plausible at the same time.

In the Ark Tablet record, the ark was actually described as being round in shape. This tablet records the following:

> Draw out the boat you will make on a circular plan:
> Let her length and breadth be equal.
> Let her floor area be one field. Let her sides be one nindan high
> I set in place thirty ribs
> Which were one parsiktu-vessel thick, ten nindan long.[128]

A ROUND ARK

The idea of a round ark has some biblical precedence. The Hebrew word used to describe the ark is *tevah*. This word is only used one other time in the Bible, to describe the basket in which the infant Moses was placed on the Nile River.[129]

A case has been made that translations for the dimensions of the ark from Babylonian could have resulted in some misinterpretation. The authors of the book *New Mathematical Cuneiform Texts* state,

> The length of the arc of the semicircle is simply called uš [in Babylonian] "length," possibly because uš was routinely used as the name for the unknown in Old Babylonian quadratic equations. In Old Babylonian, the word uš for "length" could be used to

describe the circumference of a circle or the arc length of a semicircle.[130]

Regarding the word radius, the authors state, "From a linguistic point of view, the use of Akkadian matnu 'string', is an Old Babylonian word for 'radius'. No word for 'radius' has ever appeared before in any known mathematical cuneiform text..."[131]

Author Michael Lind states that the Babylonian term for radius was obscure "even for Babylonians," which led to the concept of radius being lost in translation.[132]

RADIUS OF THE LOST ARK

Based on this theory, the size and shape of the ark would have been much different than it is conventionally conceived today. The ark's length of three hundred cubits would instead become a circumference of three hundred cubits (four hundred fifty feet). Its width of fifty cubits would become a radius of fifty cubits (seventy-five feet). Thus, the ark would be shaped like a huge bowl with a depth of thirty cubits (forty-five feet) with a total surface area equal to $\pi(r)^2$ or 3.14 times 75^2, or 17,662 square feet. Built to three floors, as per the Bible, this would give it a total of roughly fifty thousand square feet.

By comparison, a rectangular ark would have an area of 33,750 square feet (450 times 75). Thus a round ark would have been only fifty-two percent of the area a rectangular ark (17,662 divided by 33,750).

Although still large, a round ark of these dimensions would be much smaller than conventionally believed. If the flood was local, there would no longer be any need to fit two of every species in the world into the ark. Rather, only animals native to the Mesopotamian region would be included. This means the ark could be smaller and still get the job done. Also, it would be much more plausible that Noah and his sons could have built it.

Now we come to an interesting juncture regarding the dimensions of the ark. If we stipulate that the radius of the ark was fifty cubits, then based on the formula to determine a circle's circumference—2(π)r—then the circumference of the ark should be 314 cubits (two times [3.14] times fifty). But the Bible records the length (circumference) as three hundred cubits. If the dimensions given actually describe a circle, why is there a discrepancy?

To address this question, I refer to 1 Kings 7:23, which describes a cylindrical vessel built at the order of Solomon: *"He made the Sea of cast metal, circular in shape, measuring ten cubits from rim to rim and five cubits high. It took a line of thirty cubits to measure around it."* The phrase "rim to rim" describes the diameter of the vessel. The radius then would be half of that, or five.

In this passage, we have the very same relative dimensions as the ark, only reduced by ten times. To me, it is very interesting that there happens to be such a close parallel of dimensions referenced in the Bible. But the main point is that when we calculate the actual circumference of this vessel, it comes to 31.4 cubits, not thirty cubits. The circumference value here of thirty is the result of a rounding of numbers. In the same way, the circumference of the ark is rounded out for ease of communication.

Thus, I have established a biblical precedent for the concept we have introduced.

Based on this review, it is very possible that Noah's ark was round and considerably smaller than conventionally envisioned. This makes the biblical narrative seem more realistic and much more plausible to conceive.

ANIMALS ON THE ARK

Now let's talk about the animals taken onto the ark. A regional flood would only require animals native to the Mesopotamian delta to be rescued. This would be a much more realistic undertaking than collecting and accommodating all species on the Earth. It would also require a much smaller ark, as I have suggested. The logistics of the animals making their way to the ark can also be more realistically reconciled.

In Genesis 7:8 we read, *"Pairs of clean and unclean animals, of birds and of all creatures that move along the ground, male and female, came to Noah and entered the ark..."*

First of all, the shorter distances related to a local flood would have made it much more feasible for the animals to travel to the ark. And the animals are specifically said to have made their way to the ark voluntarily, as opposed to Noah capturing them.

Scientists have long observed that animals have special survival instincts and can know in advance when, for example, there will be a disaster. Along these lines, during the 2004 tsunami in the Indian Ocean, elephants broke chains to flee to higher ground hours before the tsunami hit the shoreline.[133]

Also, Yale University uses sensors to collect data from animals to provide early warning on changing environmental conditions.[134]

It is quite conceivable that God endowed animals with the instinct to know that a flood disaster was imminent, leading them to seek shelter in the ark.

THE TIMING OF THE FLOOD

When did the flood occur? This is an important question. The flood, like all events in the Bible, is recorded as happening at a specific location and at a particular time in history.

For example, Daniel's early life and prophetic career occurred during the time of the Babylonian captivity. The ministry of Christ occurred in Palestine two thousand years ago. Creation itself is described as occurring within a six-day timeframe that ended after the creation of Adam and Eve.

Thus, the events of the Bible are embedded in history and can be correlated and validated through archaeology and written records related to associated locations and times.

To the extent that it is possible regarding the flood, I will attempt to do the same.

As a starting point, a primary source for dating the flood is the Bible itself. There are two main versions of the Old Testament: the Masoretic Text (MT) and the Greek Septuagint (LXX).

The MT version is the one found in most modern Bibles. Based on the MT genealogies from Adam to Noah, as recorded in Genesis, the flood has been calculated to have occurred around 2350 BC, although other chronologies show some variations.[135]

An older flood date is derived from the LXX, which is based on Hebrew texts that are twelve centuries older than the texts upon which the MT is based. Debate exists as to which version is superior, but the LXX appears to have fewer alterations from the Dead Sea scrolls.[136]

In the LXX, the genealogies of the patriarchs span a longer time-frame. This is because the recorded ages of the patriarchs at the birth of their sons are consistently older by one hundred years.

For example, in the LXX Adam was 230 years old when Seth was born, but in the MT Adam was 130 years old. Likewise, the LXX states that Seth was 205 when Enosh was born but the MT states that he was 105.

When all the necessary genealogical age adjustments are included, the LXX provides a flood date of approximately 3300 BC compared to the MT date of approximately 2450 BC. The LXX also pushes back the creation of Adam to 5554 BC compared to the MT date of 4004 BC.[137]

Interestingly, many ancient scholars believed these older dates were correct. For example, in Eupolmus wrote 158 BC that Adam was created in 5307 BC. Josephus, the Jewish historian, estimated a date of 5467 BC. Philip of Alexander in 30 AD gave a date of 5500 BC. Many others provided similar timeframes.[138]

This suggests that a more ancient flood date has some historical as well as scriptural support. Also, a flood date of 3300 BC places this event in a geologic and anthropologic era that is associated with evidence of a massive flood. Based on a number of cross-referenced dates which will be reviewed, the LXX flood dates appear to be more accurate, in my estimation.

There was a Mesopotamian flood around 3500 BC called the great flood of Ur. The remains of this flood were discovered by Leonard Woolley in 1929. He found a layer of flood sediment eleven feet thick underneath the tombs from the Early Dynastic period. Beneath this layer of sediment, he found artifacts from a late prehistoric period. Then, beneath this layer, he encountered no indication of civilization. At the time, there was a strong belief that this archaeological find was related to Noah's flood.[139]

However, confidence in this conclusion weakened when evidence of other floods was unearthed. In addition, the date of the great flood of Ur didn't seem to properly cross-reference with other documents, including the Masoretic Text, which dates the flood to around 2300 BC.

The very idea of Noah's flood being just a local flood in Mesopotamia also wasn't well received by some Christians.

Other possible candidates for Noah's flood have included a flood at Shuruppak dated from 2950 to 2850 BC. There were other floods in the Kish area from 2900 BC to 2600 BC. Many scholars specializing in the ancient Near East have concluded that the flood stories of cuneiform literature and the Bible find their ultimate origin in the event attested to by the remains at Kish and Shuruppak. This site has attracted attention because, according to the Mesopotamian legend, Shuruppak was the home of Ziusudra, the Sumerian Noah.[140]

However, the extent of these flood deposits isn't that impressive. The Kish flood deposits average less than ten inches and at Shuruppak the deposits are about fifteen inches deep. These modest sedimentary remains are not what would be expected of a major flood that wiped out civilization. In fact, evidence exists that other cities and buildings survived these floods.

Again, based on the MT, various biblical chronologies estimate that the flood occurred between 2300–2450 BC, which is later than any of the floods mentioned. There is a lack of physical evidence for Noah's flood at this time and no evidence of a discontinuity of civilization in this timeframe.

Based on the evidence reviewed, my belief is that Noah's flood occurred around 3300 BC, or earlier. This date range aligns with the LXX and the great flood of Ur, as well as other historical events and documents.

The Bible states that Noah had a son named Ham, who became the founder of Egypt, which is referred to several times in the Bible as the land of Ham (Psalm 78:51, 105:23, 1 Chronicles 4:40). The pyramids of Egypt and tombs of Egyptian kings are dated to 2700 BC, suggesting that the flood and dispersion after the tower of Babel must have preceded this date.[141]

An earlier flood date, 3300 BC, also makes more sense and allows more time for the human population to be re-established after the flood. This includes wide dispersion to other countries, as well as the establishment of countless cities and the construction of ziggurats and pyramids in the second century BC.

SUMMARY

To summarize, there is evidence for the flood provided by:

1. The biblical testimony.
2. Legends of the flood from around the world.

3. Many independent documents validating the flood, such as the Gilgamesh Epic and the Atrahasis flood story recorded on the Wendell Prism and elsewhere.
4. The cuneiform Ark Tablet.
5. Historical cross-references of events related to the flood.
6. A confirmed physical location that is conducive to a flood of biblical proportions.

Based on all this, there is reason to conclude that Noah's flood occurred in Mesopotamia somewhere around 3300 BC, with the caveat that much is still unknown. Whatever its exact date, in light of the principles of geology and other supporting evidence, Noah's flood cannot be easily dismissed as fiction, as some might be inclined to believe. In fact, a plausible basis exists to consider the scriptural narrative to be entirely true.

Based on the evaluation criteria used in this book, Noah's flood can be seen to agree with science and also be consistent with a plausible, literal interpretation of scripture.

Twenty-Six

DARKNESS TO LIGHT AND THE ETERNAL DAY

> Every good and perfect gift is from above, coming
> down from the Father of the heavenly lights...
> (James 1:17)

DURING THE PROCESS of developing the models used in this book to validate the week-within-a-week creation model, I have identified an interesting and important commonality. I've found that all the models studied are associated with profound outcomes.

MODEL	OUTCOME
Jericho Model	Victory in the Promised Land
Daniel's 70 Weeks Model	Victorious millennial reign of Christ
Wilderness Model	Victorious entrance into the Promised Land

The themes of God's victory, the fulfillment of his promises, and eternal peace for humanity are central to all these models. In my view, these strong, unifying themes add credibility to the presented models and validate the reality and focus of the whole program of God as revealed in scripture.

I would like to further reflect on other patterns that have already been identified. Earlier, we learned that rabbinical Jewish law defines the day and night as twelve hours each, with the new day starting in the evening. We also noted that the creation days in the Genesis narrative were each punctuated at their end by evening and morning.

In many examples like this, we have observed a pattern that seems to span the entire plan of God. I call this the darkness-to-light cycle. I believe there may be an important parallel found between this cycle and the evenings and subsequent darkness at the end of each creation day before the next morning dawned.

We know from science that the universe is consigned to decay based on the second law of thermodynamics, which stipulates,

> The state of entropy of the entire universe, as an isolated system, will always increase over time. Entropy is a measure of randomness or disorder in a system, including heat loss and decay. Entropy means that over time, decay is inevitable in a stand-alone system.[142]

This concept of decay is also described in Romans 8:21: *"the creation itself will be liberated from its bondage to decay and brought into the freedom and glory of the children of God."* In addition, Colossians 1:17 asserts, *"He is before all things, and in him all things hold together."* This verse states, I suggest, that the universe would in some way fall apart without the active intervention of God in Christ.

Based on these observations, this process of decay and God's role in upholding the universe may have specific relevance to the evening and darkness which follow each creation day. The universe started in darkness, as did the Earth.

When we look at our UCW Model, the length of each day was 2.16 billion years. This leaves a very long period for the onset of decay and disorder. This increasing disorder and its natural march to entropic death could also plausibly represent darkness or night.

We read in 1 John 1:5, *"God is light; in him there is no dark-ness at all."* And as I discussed in Chapter Fifteen, each creative activity described in Genesis was preceded by the statement, "And God said…" Therefore, I suggest that during the "nights" of entro-pic decay, God introduced new commands in order to bring order and life to the universe. His creative acts didn't prevent the onset of entropy and he undoubtedly also used the forces of entropy for his purposes.

My belief is that his creative acts were accomplished through the forces of decay, despite them, or in direct opposition to them. Similar to how the Earth still turns, our crops still grow, and our children still develop while we sleep at night, God allowed the course of nature to do his bidding even during his inactivity. Then, through new inter-ventions on each creation day, God renewed the darkness-to-light cycle.

The need for his interventions didn't cease after man entered the picture. Perhaps it increased.

Such reflections cannot be proven and are expressions of faith rather than facts. Still, there is beauty and elegance in the thought of God performing his will in this way, as Lord of all. No one can perceive how God accomplishes his will, but everyone can see that wherever God goes, and in whatever he does, there is beauty, won-der, and goodness.

Please indulge me as I attempt to present this idea of the dark-ness-to-light cycle in figurative language.

THE ETERNAL DAWN

In the beginning, the stage is completely dark. There is no light; there are no actors. An empty hall full of black space awaits the start of a grand play. The theatre is barren and cold.

Suddenly, light pierces the darkness, floodlights from heaven. Soon, the pitch-black ceiling is filled with the glow of heavenly lights, and the grand theatre comes into view in all its glory. The stars shine through space at the advent of time. The curtain rises.

We see a lifeless lump of round clay suspended and wrapped in black clouds and buried beneath deep, cold water. There is no light to pierce the night and bring the dawn. There is no heat to warm its celestial frame. There is only eternal night in endless orbit.

Through the thickness of the sky, a soft and gentle glimmer appears. Almost imperceptibly, the clouds begin to lighten, dispersing a soft glow across the faceless land. As the stage slowly turns, darkness descends on one side and light appears on the other. A new stage is set. The first rays of the sun are a heavenly light dawning on the genesis of life.

Mankind ascends, new actors on the stage, bringing stories of drama and dreams to the cosmos. Yet there is darkness all about. Their minds are clouded and corrupt. A promising story quickly descends into a nightmare of cruelty and destruction. The stage is facing ruin. The director yells, "Cut!"

A lifeboat is constructed and a handful of faithful actors are cast as sailors. The stage is a watery world. A deluge of rain descends as waves of judgment crash in deadly turbulence around their craft. This floating cradle is all that lies between them and a cold and watery death.

The storm is endless. In a wilderness of eternal water, hope is washed away, like the lifeless bodies of those who turned from the light. The shipbound remnant can only yearn for the day when they once again set their feet on land that is firm and dry. There's nothing now but to endure. And then, suddenly, it happens: the sky clears, the seas calm, and the storm ceases.

Upon that dawn, gathered on the ship, the actors dream of a new world while the old one still lies soaked and crushed beneath them. They look to the sky. And there, shining in brilliant colour, is a magnificent rainbow that extends from horizon to horizon and up to the heavens. It is of divine brilliance, the likes of which has never been seen before and will never be seen again. It is a new day, with the promise of hope. The rainbow is a heavenly light, bridging the gap between light and darkness, between heaven and earth.

A new act begins on the plains below a mountain, where a man is called to make a nation. This nation escapes enslavement only to be imprisoned by wilderness. In the desert, the people are guided by a pillar of fire, a heavenly light, a beacon of a Promised Land. But still they cling to the dark ways of the past as though that is all they know.

The man ascends a mountain on a quest for the words of heaven. Approaching the mountaintop, he finds a bush on fire that shines, not burns. It is a heavenly light for a new age of enlightenment.

The nation conquers the land and puts fear into the hearts of their enemies. Their temple is built, but as time passes all the divine words are broken, like the stone tablets on which they were inscribed. The nation descends into darkness.

Now the stage is quiet, but oppression is thick in the air. Soft sounds are heard. In the stillness of night, a newborn stirs. High above, an angelic star shines bright and clear. All who gaze upon it are touched by grace and filled with wonder, like those who behold the child. This heavenly light beams earthward upon the Light of the World.

The stage lights dim. The new setting is the future, at a time when all that came before has been lost to memory. The nations yearn for a better world and seek peace. It escapes them. Fear and hate cripple all and darkness descends. The hall becomes as black as it was at the very beginning.

Suddenly, the whole theatre explodes with blinding, fearsome light. It is a heavenly light, appearing as lightning, flashing from one end of the stage to the other. There is a battle on stage and destruction everywhere, not by water but by fire. The fierce blaze consumes all the darkness.

Then stillness and peace embrace the stage. And just like that, the theatrical production ends; the play is complete. But the light remains brightly shining, never again to be quenched. The eternal light has finally, and forever, vanquished the night.

Conclusion

UNITED IN THE SEARCH

> You don't get unity by ignoring the questions that
> have to be asked.[143] —Jay Weatherill

IN THIS BOOK, I have introduced and sought to validate the week-within-a-week creation model. I am confident that this theory provides the best possible reconciliation of scripture with science. I do not present this book as being the truth in itself. Rather, it is a synthesis of ideas which provide a plausible and previously unconsidered theory about what really happened.

When it comes to determining what is scientifically true, the discovery process matters. For the scientist, that process is the scientific method. The methodology I have used, that of biblical patterns and precedents, is systematic, and I believe it too provides a solid foundation for discovery. The week-within-a-week creation model is built on four pillars:

1. The precedents provided by relevant biblical models.
2. Logical deduction relating to the Genesis narrative.
3. Calculation of the timeframes of the creation days based solely on biblical references.

4. The matching of our model's timeframes to those of natural history.

My expectation is that the week-within-a-week creation model will stand up to future scrutiny. In addition, if this model is reviewed in light of Occam's razor, I believe it provides the simplest yet most effective explanation that has yet been presented for reconciling science and scripture. This only adds to its overall appeal and credibility.

It is my sincere hope that this book will be a unifying influence for religious folks of all kinds. It is possible that proponents of twenty-four-hour days might find in it a new scriptural way to interpret the days of Genesis. If so, they may become more accepting of the findings of science without having to make concessions in their faith as to the inerrancy of scripture.

Perhaps this book will provide benefit to advocates of the day-age theory as well, as my theory shows how God has counted and divided each day of creation in the same way he knows each star by name and counts each grain of sand on the shore. For the agnostic, I hope the ideas in this book will renew respect for and spur new interest in the things of God, which can perhaps be perceived and believed after all.

This book could also be helpful for those who call themselves theistic evolutionists. If my thesis is correct and the Bible is infallible and trustworthy, scripture can be read literally, where applicable. For example, it may now be possible for theistic evolutionists to see Adam as an actual person and the Genesis narrative to be in alignment with science. This is important because it would increase the harmony between the testimony of nature and the testimony of God's Word, and such alignment can only lead to increased faith for all.

If the Bible can be understood in a way that is consistent with science, and if it substantiates known facts, perhaps the scientific community will become more open-minded toward the scriptures and the ways in which the Bible can fill the gaping void that science cannot.

Science does its thing well. But as much as science helps us understand the laws of the universe and biology, and how these laws explain the natural world, it still cannot explain how these laws first came into being. And it's not just a question of where the laws and finetuning of the universe originated. It is also a question of how mankind came to be endowed with the capacity to understand the infinitely complex language of the universe as expressed in mathematics and physics—and more than that, how we have been gifted with the ability to understand the language of art and love and the unseen spirit world, and even the language of the eternal mind of God.

So my hope is that rather than being consigned to an adversarial relationship, science and scripture can become respected partners. Each can contribute a different framework of knowledge so together they can reveal truth in all its beauty, wonder, and breadth.

God has designed creation so that it is possible to perceive him and appreciate him through faith rather than through absolute proof. It is possible to look at the world and still deny his existence if we so choose. As Hebrews 11:3 says, *"By faith we understand that the universe was formed at God's command, so that what is seen was not made out of what is visible."*

This means that the righteousness through faith (Romans 3:22) which God desires can only be achieved by an act of will, through a belief of the heart, and by a willingness to be vulnerable by trusting the unseen because we intuitively sense that it is good and true and greater than ourselves. In doing so, we find God there. This is a place where science cannot go.

Now that I have presented the week-within-a-week creation model, it's time to ask this question: what are the next steps to further investigate and validate this theory?

The first thing that comes to mind is to conduct additional work on understanding the timelines of the history of life within the timelines put forward by the model, particularly in regard to the appearance of plants and birds.

It would also be interesting to respond to feedback from the scientific and theological communities regarding the presented model and overall thesis.

In addition, it will be instructive to observe the degree to which this book will serve as an effective apologetic tool by bringing renewed attention to this subject and enhancing the credibility of biblical testimony.

Finally, we are keen to learn how well this book helps to affirm the faith of Christians everywhere.

In conclusion, my hope is that we can all eventually meet at the centre and gather around the one who created all things and in whom all things hold together. He is the Light of the World to whom all people are drawn, no matter what scientific or theological road they currently walk.

I believe this old Irish benediction is a fitting way to end this book: "May the blessings of light be upon you, light without and light within. May the blessed sunlight shine on you and warm your heart till it glows like a great peat fire."

Appendix One

TIME DILATION

> When forced to summarize the general theory
> of relativity in one sentence: Time and space
> and gravitation have no separate existence from
> matter.[144] —Albert Einstein

SEVERAL APPROACHES TAKEN by both scientists and theologians suggest ways to reconcile God's time with human time in order to make sense of the Genesis narrative. In this appendix, I will discuss one of those approaches: time dilation theory.

In discussions about the creation of the universe, it isn't unusual to hear people comment, "God's time is not like man's time." The concept that God is somehow above and outside of time is one that makes sense to most people on an intuitive level, even though it cannot be truly comprehended. A number of books have been written seeking to explain the apparently vast difference in time between the six days of creation reported in Genesis and the 13.8-billion-year age of the universe as measured by astronomy. Some of these attempts have appealed to the concept of time dilation to explain it.

Time dilation occurs when the relative velocities of two frames of reference in the universe are very high. The idea is that for an observer who is outside our frame of reference, like God, time could be experienced at a much different rate than we experience it ourselves.

By way of background, let's remember that time requires space and matter to exist. Einstein's theory of general relativity proves that space and space-time cannot exist apart from matter and energy, which create a gravitational field. The proposition that God created all matter in the universe therefore entails the corollary conclusion that God also created time. Support for this proposition is found in 1 Corinthians 2:7: *"we declare God's wisdom, a mystery that has been hidden and that God destined for our glory before time began."*

Einstein's theory of special relativity has been thoroughly validated over the past one hundred years through repeated experiments. One of the key features of special relativity is the observation of time dilation resulting from the relative velocity between different frames of reference.

So what does this mean? It means that if you were standing at the edge of the expanding universe (picture standing on the surface of a balloon as it is being inflated), you would experience time at a slower rate than someone who was standing on the Earth (inside the balloon).

Basically, there is greater time dilation as the speed between the two frames of reference approaches the speed of light. Theoretically, time stops when two objects are moving away from each other at the speed of light.

While interesting, time dilation cannot explain the vast difference in time between six twenty-four-hour days of creation and 13.8 billion years of evolution. The universe would have to be expanding at virtually the speed of light (300,000 kilometres per second) to do this compared to the actual measured speed of seventy-three kilometres per second.

Based on the speed of the expansion of the universe, time would slow down for the observer, but only slightly. Time would be approximately ninety-seven percent of normal, which adds up to a difference of eleven days per year rather than the factors of billions required to provide reconciliation.

In addition, while an observer who is on the edge of the expanding universe would experience time passing more slowly, time on the Earth would pass in the usual manner. So the long-acting geologic and biological processes which occurred here on the Earth still required millions or billions of years as measured by the geological, paleontological, and astronomical records.

It would therefore not be credible, based on time dilation theory, to argue that the Earth is only six thousand years old and the creation process occurred in six twenty-four-hour days.

What value does the theoretical framework of time dilation add to the discussion of the creation narrative? In my opinion, it reinforces the idea that God's perspective of timeframes and his frame of reference are different and above ours. It's impossible to put God into a box defined by our limited experience and comprehension of space and time. Also, time dilation is another example of the intricacy of the universe and how it is inexplicably governed by complex mathematical relationships.

In summary, this review of time dilation provides support for the idea that the universe was created in marvellous ways. But time dilation does not provide an explanation for the days of Genesis.

Appendix Two

BIRDS AND DINOSAURS

> A goose flies by a chart the Royal Geographic
> Society could not improve.[145] — Oliver Wendell
> Holmes Jr.

I INTRODUCE HERE an interpretation of the appearance of birds in an attempt to reconcile the fossil record with God's creative activity on day five.

In Genesis 1:20, God announced his intention to create birds: *"Let the water teem with living creatures, and let birds fly above the earth across the vault of the sky."* In the next verse we read,

> So God created the great creatures of the sea and every living thing with which the water teems and that moves about in it, according to their kinds, and every winged bird according to its kind. And God saw that it was good. (Genesis 1:21)

As mentioned in Chapter Eighteen, day five spans the period from 720 million years ago to 360 million years ago. Therefore, according to my theory, birds should have appeared in this timeframe. However, the oldest discovered bird fossils are approximately 160 million years old.

The problem of birds being created on the same day as fish will arise in any possible creation week theory which hopes to align itself with the fossil record. This is because fish first appeared more than five hundred million years ago, in the middle of day five of our model. There is, therefore, an apparent time gap between the appearance of fish and birds, although both were created on day five of the Genesis narrative.

One suggested explanation for this anomaly relates to the observation that there is a strong biological link between reptiles, dinosaurs, and birds. Evolutionists have concluded that birds descended from theropods. Whatever one's belief about origins, the morphologies of dinosaurs, theropods, reptiles, crocodilians, and birds are closely linked. They share many anatomical features to the extent that birds are anatomically classified as being dinosaurs under the broad classification of archosaurs.[146]

Dinosaurs, reptiles, and theropods all laid hard-shelled eggs, like birds. In addition, dinosaurs had feathers.

According to John P. Rafferty, writing for Britannica, "One of the most surprising developments in paleontology in recent years has been the discovery that, like birds, dinosaurs—many dinosaurs, in fact—possessed feathers.

Using modern spectrometry, paleontologists have shown that feathers on dinosaurs were well-developed and sometimes even irradiant. The scales and feathers of all archosaurs, including birds, are made of beta-keratin. The teeth and bone structures are also similar within this category.[147]

There is no specific mention in the Genesis narrative of dinosaurs. As dinosaurs had long been extinct at the time Genesis was written, references to dinosaurs would not have been meaningful to readers until modern times. Dinosaurs appeared 240 million years ago and the first land vertebrates preceding dinosaurs were tetrapods. Archosaurs were a clade of tetrapods which appeared about 397 million years ago in the middle of the Devonian period.[148] This would fall within the timeframe of day five in our model.

It may therefore have been the case that, in the brief Genesis narrative, dinosaurs and theropods were included by God in the broad category of birds. In other words, if Genesis had recorded that archosaurs were created on day five, rather than birds, the narrative would align closely. And because birds are archosaurs, this could justify doing so. But then again, the word archosaur would have had no meaning to readers until relatively recently.

We have noted that Genesis 1:20 says, *"Let birds fly above the earth across the face of the sky."* Therefore, a plain reading of the text would appear not to speak of dinosaurs. However, attempts have been made to address this by pointing out the text of Genesis 1:22, where God says, *"Let the birds increase on the earth."* The possible implication here is that these "birds" were already on the Earth; that is, they were dinosaurs on the ground and not yet in the air. It's not until day six, in Genesis 1:26, that God makes reference to *"the birds in the sky."* Note that Genesis 1:22 does not say, "Let the birds of the air multiply on the earth." The distinction here could be important. If the creation of birds started on day five and then *"the birds of the air"* eventually appeared on day six of our model, this would match the fossil record. This theory may thus warrant consideration.

QUESTIONS ABOUT ADAM

> The divine spark leaps from the finger of God to the
> finger of Adam, whether it takes ultimate shape in
> a law of physics or a law of the land, a poem or a
> policy, a sonata or a mechanical computer.[149]
> — Alfred Whitney Griswold

I NOW WISH to examine a number of scripture passages pertaining to the creation of Adam which have caused confusion over the years. First, Genesis 2:5 says, *"Now no shrub had yet appeared on the earth, and no plant had yet sprung up, for the Lord God had not sent rain on the earth..."* Young Earth creationists interpret this passage to mean that it had never rained on the Earth until this time. Such a belief is based on the idea that the Earth was then only six days old.

But of course that theory doesn't conform to science. I suggest that the meaning of this verse is different: in the immediate vicinity, there had not been rain since the recent creation of the Garden of Eden. Perhaps the region, other than the rivers, was desert-like.

The same passage continues to say that *"there was no one to work the ground"* (Genesis 2:5). This has traditionally been taken to mean that there were no other people on the Earth.

I would suggest that a possible and perhaps more logical reading of this passage would be that there was no one with sophisticated agricultural skills to farm the area. This is important. If Adam was real and relatively recently created, this would be the timeframe when we would see an increase in the level of farming sophistication among hominids.

Nathan Murphy and Christopher Sailus have written,

> The earliest evidence of a Mesopotamian plow came from the Sumerians around 4000–3000 BCE... Mesopotamian civilization began over 6000 years ago, in the area of land between the Tigris and Euphrates rivers.[150]

Readers may recall that the land between the Tigris and Euphrates rivers is where the Garden of Eden is said to be situated in Genesis 2:13–14.

This theory must consider other questions in Genesis. Who did the sons of Adam marry? Why was Cain afraid of others who might kill him (Genesis 4:14)? For whom was Cain going to build a city (Genesis 4:17)?

The prior and concurrent existence of other members of the Homo sapiens species makes these references somewhat more sensible. This is seen to support my thesis. Adam was the first man, as defined by the Bible, given capabilities to enable a personal relationship with God. But Adam was not the first Homo sapiens on the Earth. I am comfortable saying this because, based on the scriptural precedents established in this book, it was not necessary for Adam and Eve to have been the first of their species.

Adam and Eve were special creations of God, unique and the first of their kind, like the nation of Israel and Jesus. Similarly, after receiving the law of Moses and entering the Promised Land, the Israelites took a giant step forward in terms of their knowledge of God compared to their predecessors and neighbours. Jesus was orders of magnitude superior to the men of Galilee and the rest of humanity.

In this light, it makes sense for Adam to represent a similar quantum leap in the creation story of mankind.

Another way to look at this is to compare the creation of the Earth to the creation of Homo sapiens. In Genesis 1:2, the Earth is described as *"formless and empty."* The Brown-Driver-Briggs Lexicon explains,

> The words "without form" and "void" are translations of the Hebrew words *tohu* and *bohu*. *Toho* and *bohu* are often paired together in the Old Testament and portray a "place of chaos, formlessness, emptiness, a wasteland."[151]

It is from this state that God begins his creative work, transforming the Earth into a garden of life. I suggest that hominids before Adam may have been like a wasteland, void of a covenant relationship with God.

The framework of creation in the Bible is revealed to be punctuated and driven by supernatural interventions by God into the natural world and the affairs of man. Scientific study confirms this dynamic, where relatively sudden developments have occurred within the context of the general uniformity of natural processes.

I believe that God's special creative intervention in regard to Adam changed the future of mankind. It was done at just the right time. It was a defining moment, a decisive action, just like all the other creative acts of God in Genesis.

The concept of God's special creations coming at just the right time is not without precedent. In Romans 5:6, Paul says, *"You see, at just the right time, when we were still powerless, Christ died for the ungodly."* The same could be said for Israel. The nation of Israel was necessary for the message of Jesus to be understood in relation to the law of Moses, and in terms of the feasts and the whole Torah.

What is important to note here is the pattern of God defining history through his special formations, brought into being at just the right time. This is a model for how his creative actions have ultimately controlled the natural dynamics of the universe and the Earth over long periods of time. This model supports both an old creation and yet one that God totally controls.

SCIENTIFIC ARGUMENTS AGAINST A GLOBAL FLOOD

> The facts are always friendly, every bit of evidence
> one can acquire, in any area, leads one that much
> closer to what is true.[152] — Carl Rogers

THE BELIEF THAT Noah's flood covered the entire globe is a view still held by young Earth creationists, but it faces many serious challenges from science and common sense arguments. In Chapter Nine, I presented a few examples of evidence that confirm the Earth to be millions of years old.

Below, I provide additional evidence that a global flood isn't scientifically tenable. Note that this list is much abbreviated compared to all the evidence available.

The amount of water required to cover the entire globe, including all the mountains, does not exist. All the water vapour in the sky represents only .001 percent of the Earth's water and wouldn't make any material difference to the amount of water involved in a global flood.[153]

Where would the vast amount of water involved in a global flood drain to, and how long would it take to evaporate? The explanation given by young Earth creationists is that massive tectonic activity occurred globally during the flood, creating all the mountain peaks on the Earth and separating the continents by thousands of miles in a period of one year. The rising of these landforms thus allowed drainage after the flood.

However, science has established that these tectonic process-es occurred over hundreds of millions of years. There is also no evidence of the creation of mountain peaks in the flood narrative. Furthermore, tectonic action moving continents thousands of miles apart and creating so many mountain peaks in such a compressed span of time would be unsurvivable even to those on the ark due to tsunamis. The heat and toxicity of such volcanic and tectonic action and the weight of the water would also have generated 10^{28} joules of heat, enough "to boil most of the oceans and melt the earth's rocks."[154]

A global flood would cause all freshwater and saltwater to mix, killing most fish. The vast majority of fish need to remain in their nat-ural habitat defined by temperature, depth of water, and food sourc-es. One might also wonder how the freshwater fish could ever again find their natural habitats when the flood receded.[155]

In Genesis 7:2–3, Noah is told to take pairs of all animals into the ark with him. Then God says, *"Seven days from now I will send rain on the earth for forty days and forty nights, and I will wipe from the face of the earth every living creature I have made"* (Genesis 7:4). How could millions of creatures from across oceans and from far-away islands get to the ark at all, let alone in seven days? And how, after the flood was over, could these creatures return to their natural habitat, be it in Madagascar or Australia or whatever single habitat some animals need to survive?

There seems no plausible way that eight people could care for the literally millions of species of animals that exist in the world.[156]

There is a geologic area called the Green River Formation in Wyoming that covers tens of thousands of square miles. It contains about twenty million thin layers of sediment, called verves, alternating fine and dark, each pair representing seasonal sedimentary deposits. These deposits were laid down over the course of approximately twenty-three million years. It's not possible for twenty million separate strata to have been created through the flow of floodwater over the course of less than a year during the flood.[157]

The geology of the Grand Canyon could not have been formed by Noah's flood. For example, the erosion rate of Zoraster granite has been calculated to be one-thousandth of an inch per year. The deep erosion of the canyon would therefore have had to take millions of years.[158]

Also, the levels of sedimentary rock lining the canyon form a smooth, stair-stepped appearance caused by erosion over long periods of time. These layers would not have had time to harden to form cliffs had they all been laid down simultaneously.[159]

On all continents, fossils are found in sedimentary rock which are separated by many layers of evaporite rock salt, magnesium, and potash that turn a reddish colour only when they dry. These layers can be more than a kilometre thick. Thus the different layers of fossils were laid down only after other huge volumes of sediments were deposited and then dried.

In the case of a global flood causing fossilization, there would have been no opportunity for the multiple flooding and drying cycles required to create this common type of geologic formation. It is also the case that ninety-nine percent of fossils are extinct animals, which doesn't fit with all animals surviving the flood four to five thousand years ago.[160]

In addition, earlier forms of life, such as trilobites, are invariably found in the oldest and deepest sediment, whereas the more recent lifeforms are found in the upper strata. Between these many fossil layers are other sedimentary strata formed over millions of years. There is no evidence in the fossil record of a very recent extinction event.

After the rain stopped, Noah released a dove which later returned to the ark with a fresh olive twig in its beak. Olive trees have been shown to die if submerged for more than three months. This infers that the whole world could not have been submerged for a year for the olive tree to have survived the flood.[161]

ENDNOTES

1 Albert Einstein and Leopold Infeld, The Evolution of Physics (Cambridge, UK: Cambridge University Press, 1938), 159.

2 Walter Cronkite, "In seeking truth..." Goodreads. Date of access: August 7, 2024 (https://www.goodreads.com/quotes/346861-in-seeking-truth-you-have-to-get-both-sides-of).

3 David Limbaugh, "Inerrancy Quotes," Defending Inerrancy. Date of access: July 22, 2024 (https://defendinginerrancy.com/inerrancy-quotes).

4 "The Apostles' Creed," Church of England. Date of access: August 7, 2024 (https://www.churchofengland.org/our-faith/what-we-believe/apostles-creed).

5 Christopher Nolan, "The scientific method..." Goodreads. Date of access: August 8, 2024 (https://www.goodreads.com/quotes/11760257-the-scientific-method-i-think-is-the-highest-philosophical-height).

6 René Descartes, "Rene Descartes: Scientific Method," Internet Encyclopedia of Philosophy. Date of access: July 22, 2024 (https://iep.utm.edu/descartes-scientific-method).

7 "What Is the James Webb Space Telescope?" NASA Science. Date of access: July 22, 2024 (https://webb.nasa.gov/content/about/faqs/facts.html).

8 Alice Calaprice, The Ultimate Quotable Einstein (Princeton, NJ: Princeton University Press, 2011), 103.

9 Huston Smith, Why Religion Matters: The Future of Faith in an Age of Disbelief (San Francisco, CA: Harper One, 2006), 68.

10 Sheldon Krimsky, "Do Financial Conflicts of Interest Bias Research? An Inquiry into the 'Funding Effect' Hypothesis," Science, Technology, and Human Values 38(4). September 20, 2012. 566–587.

11 Jacob Bronowski, "Science Quotes for Inquiring Minds," Keep Inspiring. Date of access: July 22, 2024 (https://www.keepinspiring.me/science-quotes).

12 B.F. Skinner, Beyond Freedom and Dignity (Cambridge, MA: Hackett Publishing, 1971).

13 "Causal Determinism," Stanford Encyclopedia of Philosophy. Date of access: July 22, 2024 (https://plato.stanford.edu/entries/determinism-causal).

14 Albert Einstein, "Science and Religion." Nature 146. November 9, 1940. 605–607.

15 Ewald M. Plass, ed., What Luther Says: A Practical In-Home Anthology for the Active Christian (St. Louis, MO: Concordia, 1959), 93.

16 Stephen W. Boyd, "Statistical Determination of Genre in Biblical Hebrew: Evidence for an Historical Reading of Genesis 1:1–2:3," Institute for Creation Research. November 1, 2005 (https://www.icr.org/article/statistical-determination-genre-biblical).

17 "Days of the Week in Hebrew," Rosen School of Hebrew. Date of access: July 23, 2024 (https://lp.rosenhebrewschool.com/lp-rosen-modern-hebrew-days_of_the_week-en.html).

18 "The Number 7 in the Bible," Bible Study Tools. November 11, 2023 (https://www.biblestudytools.com/topical-verses/the-number-7-in-the-bible).

19 "Easton's Bible Dictionary—Seven," Bible Study Tools. Date of access: August 7, 2024 (https://www.biblestudytools.com/dictionary/seven).

20 "Understanding the Sevens in Revelation," VerseNotes. April 26, 2019 (https://versenotes.org/sevens-in-revelation).

21 Rabbi Jason Sobel, "Why Does the Bible Say 7 Times 70," Fusion Global. Date of access: July 23, 2024 (https://www.fusionglobal.org/connections/why-7-times-70).

22 Edward O. Thorp, "I also learned the value…" Goodreads. Date of access: August 7, 2024 (https://www.goodreads.com/quotes/8526673-i-also-learned-the-value-of-withholding-judgement-until-i).

23 George Santayana, "The Sense of Beauty," Santayana Edition. Date of access: August 7, 2024 (https://santayana.iupui.edu/wp-content/uploads/2017/11/George-Santayana-The-Sense-of-Beauty.pdf). See page 80.

24 John Maynard Keynes, "The difficulty lies not…" Goodreads. Date of access: August 7, 2024 (https://www.goodreads.com/quotes/5099424-the-difficulty-lies-not-so-much-in-developing-new-ideas).

25 John J. Parsons, "Seven Days of History," Hebrew4Christians. Date of access: August 10, 2024 (https://hebrew4christians.com/Scripture/Parashah/Summaries/

Bereshit/Seven_Days/seven_days.html).

26 Daniel Friedmann, The Genesis Code One (Aberdeen, UK: Inspired Books, 2016), 66.

27 Albert Einstein, "The ways of creation are wrapt…" AZQuotes. Date of access: August 7, 2024 (https://www.azquotes.com/quote/1040772).

28 Nathan Leefer et al, "New Limits on Variation of the Fine-Constant Structure Constant using Atomic Dysprosium," Physical Review Letters 111. August 6, 2013.

29 "Zircon Chronology: Dating the Oldest Material on Earth," American Museum of Natural History. Date of access: July 23, 2024 (https://www.amnh.org/learn-teach/curriculum-collections/earth-inside-and-out/zircon-chronology-dating-the-oldest-material-on-earth).

30 Dr. Hugh Ross, A Matter of Days (Colorado Springs, CO: NavPress, 2015), 188.

31 E.R. Shephard-Thorn, Geology of the County Around Ramsgate and Dover (Richmond, UK: Her Majesty's Stationary Office, 1988).

32 "About Ice Cores," National Science Foundation. Date of access: July 23, 2024 (https://icecores.org/about-ice-cores).

33 Ross, A Matter of Days, 139, 237, 242.

34 Tim Elliott and Sarah T. Stewart, "Shadows Cast on Moon's Origin," Nature 504. December 5, 2013. 90–91.

35 Hugh Ross, "Moon Strike, Lunar Origin Causes 'Philosophical Disquiet,'" Salvo. Date of access: August 7, 2024 (https://salvomag.com/article/salvo29/moon-strike).

36 Ibid., 46.

37 Tim LaHaye, "You have to take…" BrainyQuote. Date of access: August 7, 2024 (https://www.brainyquote.com/quotes/tim_lahaye_240816).

38 "Prophetic Year," Academic Dictionaries and Encyclopedias. Date of access: July 23, 2024 (https://en-academic.com/dic.nsf/enwiki/6397892).

39 "The Jewish Day," Chabad. Date of access: July 23, 2024 (https://www.chabad.org/library/article_cdo/aid/526873/jewish/The-Jewish-Day.htm).

40 "Rosh Chodesh, Sanctifying the Jewish Month," Hebrew4Christians. Date of access: July 23, 2024 (https://www.hebrew4christians.com/Holidays/Rosh_Chodesh/rosh_chodesh.html).

41 "Rosh Chodashim, Nisan and the Biblical New Year," Hebrew 4 Christians. Date of access: July 23, 2024 (https://www.hebrew4christians.com/Holidays/Spring_Holi-

days/Rosh_Chodashim/rosh_chodashim.html).

42 Robert Anderson, The Coming Prince (London, UK: Hodder & Stoughton, 1894), 61.

43 Robert Anderson, The Coming Prince (London, UK: Hodder & Stoughton, 1894), 59.

44 Wayne Croley, Insights on End Times (Antelope, CA: Prophecy Proof Insights, 2022), 64.

45 Judah David Eisenstein, "Sabbatical Year and Jubilee," Jewish Encyclopedia. Date of access: July 24, 2024 (https://www.jewishencyclopedia.com/articles/8943-jubilee).

46 Rabbi Immanuel Bernstein, "The Missing Mitzvah: The Obligation of Remembering the Exodus Every Day," OU Torah. Date of access: July 24, 2024 (https://outorah. org/p/73601).

47 Rabbi Irving Greenberg, "Why the Exodus Was So Significant," My Jewish Learning. Date of access: July 24, 2024 (https://www.myjewishlearning.com/article/the-exodus-effect).

48 Bob DeWaay, "Pre-Millennialism and the Earth Church Fathers," Critical Issues Commentary Scholarly. Date of access: August 7, 2024 (https://cicministry.org/scholarly/sch008.htm).

49 Andrew Sibley, "Creation and Millennialism Among the Church Fathers," Journal of Creation 26(3). December 2012. 95–100.

50 Matthew Carey, "Chronological Index of the Years and Times from Adam unto Christ," Houston Christian University. Date of access: August 7, 2024 (https://hc.edu/museums/dunham-bible-museum/tour-of-the-museum/bible-in-america/bibles-for-a-young-republic/chronological-index-of-the-years-and-times-from-adam-unto-christ).

51 "Relative Hour (Jewish Law)," Scholarly Community Encyclopedia. Date of access: July 24, 2024 (https://encyclopedia.pub/entry/30073).

52 Thomas D. Ice, God's Purpose for Israel During the Tribulation (Lynchburg, VA: Liberty University, 2009).

53 Plato, "The beginning is the…" Goodreads. Date of access: August 7, 2024 (https://www.goodreads.com/quotes/249055-the-beginning-is-the-most-important-part-of-the-work).

54 Ross, A Matter of Days, 74.

55 "Geologic Time," Britannica. May 28, 2024 (https://www.britannica.com/science/

geologic-time).

56 "International Chronostratigraphic Chart," Stratigraphy.org. Date of access: August 7, 2024 (https://stratigraphy.org/ICSchart/ChronostratChart2012.pdf).

57 "First Land Plants and Fungi Changed Earth's Climate, Paving the Way for Explosive Evolution of Land Animals, New Gene Study Suggests," Science Daily. August 10, 2001 (https://www.sciencedaily.com/releases/2001/08/010810070021.htm).

58 Rasmus Kragh Jakobsen, "World's Oldest Fossil Plants Could Rewrite Life's Earth History," Science Nordic. March 14, 2017 (https://www.sciencenordic.com/animals--plants-denmark-evolution/worlds-oldest-fossil-plants-could-rewrite-lifes-early-history/1443668).

59 Michael Le Page, "Billion-Year-Old Fossil Seaweeds Could Be Ancestors of All Land Plants," New Scientist. February 24, 2020 (https://www.newscientist.com/article/2234683-billion-year-old-fossil-seaweeds-could-be-ancestors-of-all-land-plants).

60 "St. Augustine and Cosmology," Villanova University. Date of access: July 24, 2024 (https://www1.villanova.edu/villanova/artsci/anthro/Previous_Lectures/sustain/AugustineCosmology0.html).

61 Stephen L. Brusatte, Jingmai K. O'Connor, and Erich D. Jarvis, "The Origin and Diversification of Birds," Current Biology 25(19). October 5, 2015.

62 "Permian Extinction," Britannica. Date of access: July 24, 2024 (https://www.britannica.com/science/Permian-extinction).

63 Charles Colson, "Some have asserted..." Goodreads. Date of access: August 8, 2024 (https://www.goodreads.com/quotes/10502670-some-have-asserted-that-the-universe-was-self-generated-this-violates).

64 Embry Riddle, "New Technique More Precisely Determines the Ages of Stars," Phys.org. January 10, 2019 (https://phys.org/news/2019-01-technique-precisely-ages-stars.html).

65 David Crookes, "Methuselah: The Oldest Star in the Universe," Space. March 7, 2022 (https://www.space.com/how-can-a-star-be-older-than-the-universe.html).

66 A.S. Adikesavan, "How Do You Calculate the Age of the Universe Using the Hubble Constant?" Socratic Q&A. July 17, 2016 (https://socratic.org/questions/how-do-you-calculate-the-age-of-the-universe-using-the-hubble-constant).

67 Sasha Warren, "The Hubble Constant, Explained," The University of Chicago. Date of access: July 25, 2024 (https://news.uchicago.edu/explainer/hubble-constant-explained).

68 "Hubble Reaches New Milestone in Mystery of Universe's Expansion Rate," NASA.

May 19, 2022 (https://science.nasa.gov/centers-and-facilities/goddard/hubble-reaches-new-milestone-in-mystery-of-universes-expansion-rate).

69 "Cosmic History," NASA. Date of access: August 8, 2024 (https://science.nasa.gov/universe/overview).

70 "The End of the Cosmic Dawn," Max-Planck-Gesellschaft. June 7, 2022 (https://www.mpg.de/18720037/the-end-of-the-cosmic-dawn).

71 Dana Najjar, "The Beginning to the End of the Universe: The Cosmic Dark Ages," Astronomy. January 12, 2021 (https://www.astronomy.com/science/the-beginning-to-the-end-of-the-universe-the-cosmic-dark-ages).

72 Naomi Dinmore, "Let There Be Light: Emerging from the Cosmic Dark Ages in the Early Universe," SciTech Daily. May 3, 2023 (https://scitechdaily.com/let-there-be-light-emerging-from-the-cosmic-dark-ages-in-the-early-universe).

73 "First Law of Thermodynamics," Science Direct. Date of access: July 25, 2024 (https://www.sciencedirect.com/topics/physics-and-astronomy/first-law-of-thermodynamics).

74 Herman Pontzer, "Overview of Hominin Evolution," Nature.com. Date of access: August 8, 2024 (https://www.nature.com/scitable/knowledge/library/overview-of-hominin-evolution-89010983).

75 Brian Handwerk, "An Evolutionary Timeline of Homo Sapiens," Smithsonian. February 2, 2021 (https://www.smithsonianmag.com/science-nature/essential-timeline-understanding-evolution-homo-sapiens-180976807).

76 "Man," Merriam-Webster. Date of access: August 8, 2024 (https://www.merriam-webster.com/dictionary/man).

77 "A Conversation with Brian Greene," Nova. Date of access: August 8, 2024 (https://www.pbs.org/wgbh/nova/elegant/greene.html).

78 Dr. Dennis Bonnette, "The Scientific Possibility of Adam and Eve," Strange Notions. Date of access: July 25, 2024 (https://strangenotions.com/the-scientific-possibility-of-adam-and-eve).

79 Chris Stringer, "Are Neanderthals the Same Species as Us?" Natural History Museum. Date of access: August 8, 2024 (https://www.nhm.ac.uk/discover/are-neanderthals-same-species-as-us.html).

80 Kenneth W. Kemp, "Science, Theology, and Monogenesis," American Catholic Philosophical Quarterly 85(2). 2011. 217–236.

81 William Cowper, "God Moves in a Mysterious Way," 1774.

82 Lisa Hendry, "The Neanderthal in Us," Natural History Museum. Date of access: July 25, 2024 (https://www.nhm.ac.uk/discover/the-neanderthal-in-us.html).

83 Cecil Frances Alexander, "All Things Bright and Beautiful," 1848.

84 Alice Calaprice, ed., The Ultimate Quotable Einstein, 170.

85 Joyce Kilmer, "Trees," Poets.org. Date of access: August 8, 2024 (https://poets.org/poem/trees).

86 Robert M. Macnab, "The Bacterial Flagellum: Reversible Rotary Propeller and Type III Export Apparatus," Journal of Bacteriology 181(23). December 1999. 7149–7153.

87 Doug Corrigan, "Folding DNA," X.com. November 6, 2023 (https://x.com/Science-WDrDoug/status/1721709701048496629).

88 Nicholas Wade, "Life's Origins Get Murkier and Messier: Genetic Analysis Yields Intimations for a Primordial Commune," The New York Times. June 13, 2000 (https://www.nytimes.com/2000/06/13/science/life-s-origins-get-murkier-messier-genetic-analysis-yields-intimations.html).

89 "The Complexity of a Cell," Escola Superior de Agricultura. Date of access: July 25, 2024 (http://www.esalq.usp.br/lepse/imgs/conteudo_thumb/The-Complexity-of-the-Cell.pdf). Citing W.H. Thorpe.

90 Ibid.

91 Ibid. Citing Homer Jacobsen.

92 "Collective Cluelessness," The Skeptical Zone. April 18, 2016 (http://theskepticalzone.com/wp/collective-cluelessness).

93 Fred Hoyle, Evolution from Space: A Theory of Cosmic Creationism (New York, NY: Simon & Schuster, 1981), 24.

94 Rana, Is Darwinian Evolution Left Unexplained? 3.

95 Ibid., 2

96 Michael Sherbon, "Physical Mathematics and the Fine-Constant Structure," Journal of Advances in Physics 24(3). July 11, 2018. 5758–5764.

97 "Anthropic Principle," Britannica. July 30, 2024 (https://www.britannica.com/science/anthropic-principle).

98 Max Born, "If alpha were bigger…" Goodreads. Date of access: August 10, 2024 (https://www.goodreads.com/quotes/1016473-if-alpha-the-fine-structure-constant-were-bigger-than-it-really).

99 "The Mysterious 137," Richard Feynman. Date of access: August 10, 2024 (http://www.feynman.com/science/the-mysterious-137).

100 "Anthropic Principle," University of Oregon. Date of access: August 10, 2024 (https://pages.uoregon.edu/jschombe/cosmo/lectures/lec24.html).

101 Ibid.

102 Ibid.

103 Albert Einstein, "One may say the eternal…" BrainyQuote. Date of access: August 8, 2024 (https://www.brainyquote.com/quotes/albert_einstein_396536).

104 "Anthropic Principle," University of Oregon. Date of access: July 25, 2024 (https://pages.uoregon.edu/imamura/SCS123/lecture-1/anthropic.html).

105 Thomas Edison, "Until man duplicates…" Goodreads. Date of access: August 8, 2024 (https://www.goodreads.com/quotes/7347916-until-man-duplicates-a-blade-of-grass-nature-can-laugh).

106 Jules Henri Poincare, "Jules Henri Poincare on Unquestioning Doubt and Belief," The Hannah Arendt Center for Politics and Humanities. Date of access: August 8, 2024 (https://hac.bard.edu/amor-mundi/jules-henri-poincare-on-unquestioning-doubt-and-belief-2015-10-20).

107 "Noah," King James Bible Dictionary. Date of access: July 26, 2024 (https://king-jamesbibledictionary.com/Dictionary/Noah).

108 Frank Lorey, "The Flood of Noah and the Floor of Gilgamesh," Institute for Creation Research. March 1, 1997 (https://www.icr.org/article/noah-flood-gilgamesh).

109 "The Weld-Blundell Prism of Sumerian King List," Cuneiform Digital Library Initiative. Date of access: July 26, 2024 (https://cdli.mpiwg-berlin.mpg.de/postings/188).

110 William C. Henry, "Ancient Mesopotamia: The Sumerian King List and the Diatonic G-Scale Factor 9," The History Files. March 2015 (https://www.historyfiles.co.uk/FeaturesMiddEast/MesopotamiaSumerList02.htm).

111 Joshua J. Mark, "The Atrahasis Epic: The Great Flood and the Meaning of Suffering," Ancient History Encyclopedia. March 6, 2011 (www.ancient.eu/article/227).

112 "How to Build Noah's Ark," Archaeology.wiki. January 28, 2014 (https://www.archaeology.wiki/blog/2014/01/28/how-to-build-noahs-ark).

113 John D. Currid, Against the Gods: The Polemical Theology of the Old Testament (Wheaton, IL: Crossway, 2013), 61.

114 "What Is the Textual Basis for the Genesis 6–9 Flood Being Global?" Biblical Hermeneutics Stack Exchange. June 17, 2020 (https://hermeneutics.stackexchange.com/questions/30369/what-is-the-textual-basis-for-the-genesis-6-9-flood-being-global).

115 Ibid.

116 Lorence Collins, "Yes, Noah's Flood May Have Happened, But Not Over the Whole World," Research Gate. September 2009 (https://ncse.ngo/yes-noahs-flood-may-have-happened-not-over-whole-earth).

117 Patrick J. Kiger, "How Mesopotamia Became the Cradle of Civilization," History.com. June 20, 2023 (https://www.history.com/news/how-mesopotamia-became-the-cradle-of-civilization).

118 Steve Sarigianis, "Noah's Flood: A Bird's Eye View," Reasons to Believe. July 1, 2002 (https://reasons.org/explore/publications/facts-for-faith/noah-s-flood-a-bird-s-eye-view).

119 Ibid.

120 Jeffrey I. Rose, "New Light on Human Prehistory in the Arabo-Persian Gulf Oasis," Current Anthropology. December 2010, 849–83.

121 Ibid.

122 Steve Sarigianis, "Noah's Flood: A Bird's Eye View," Reasons. July 1, 2002 (https://reasons.org/explore/publications/facts-for-faith/noah-s-flood-a-bird-s-eye-view).

123 The Great Mississippi River Flood of 1927, National Museum of African Americans. Date of access: August 8, 2024 (https://nmaahc.si.edu/explore/stories/great-mississippi-river-flood-1927).

124 Steve Sarigianis, "Noah's Flood: A Bird's Eye View," Reasons. July 1, 2002 (https://reasons.org/explore/publications/facts-for-faith/noah-s-flood-a-bird-s-eye-view).

125 "The Egyptian Cubit: The Birth of Calibration," HBK World. Date of access: July 26, 2024 (https://www.hbkworld.com/en/knowledge/resource-center/articles/egyptian-cubit).

126 "The Wreck of the Schooner Wyoming, the Largest Wooden Ship in History," Media Monday. May 16, 2022 (https://www.hrmm.org/history-blog/media-monday-the-wreck-of-the-schooner-wyoming-the-largest-wooden-ship-in-history).

127 "Wyoming: Largest Wooden Ship Ever Built," Experience Maritime Maine. Date of access: July 26, 2024 (https://www.experiencemaritimemaine.org/portfolio/wyoming-largest-wooden-ship-ever-built-in-bath-me).

128 Nathan Wasserman, "The Flood: The Akkadian Source," Isubü Bilgi Merkezi. Date of access: July 26, 2024 (https://librarycatalog.isparta.edu.tr/vufind/Record/doab48637/Similar).

129 "Ark of Moses," Encyclopedia.com. Date of access: July 26, 2024 (https://www.encyclopedia.com/religion/encyclopedias-almanacs-transcripts-and-maps/ark-moses).

130 Joran Friberg and Farouk N.H. Al-Rawi, New Mathematical Cuneiform Texts (New York, NY: Springer Publishing, 2017), 258.

131 Ibid., 252.

132 Michael Lind, "Mystery of Noah's Ark Solved!" Tablet. July 25, 2022 (https://www.tabletmag.com/sections/news/articles/the-mystery-of-noahs-ark).

133 "The Sixth Sense: How Animals Detect Natural Disasters Before They Strike," Woke Waves. June 9, 2024 (https://www.wokewaves.com/posts/how-animals-sense-natural-disasters).

134 Bill Hathaway, "Gauging the Key Role Animals Play in Monitoring Climate Change," Yale News. September 18, 2023 (https://news.yale.edu/2023/09/18/gauging-key-role-animals-can-play-monitoring-climate-change).

135 "Chronology: Septuagint vs. Masoretic Text," Bible Topic Exposition. January 3, 2017 (https://bibletopicexpo.wordpress.com/2017/01/03/chronology-septuagint-versus-masoretic-text).

136 Rory Fox, "Septuagint or Masoretic Text: Which Is the True Version of the Bible?" Catholic Stand. June 7, 2023 (https://catholicstand.com/septuagint-or-masoretic-text-which-is-the-true-version-of-the-bible).

137 "Bible Chronology Charts," Bible.ca. November 2017 (https://www.bible.ca/manuscripts/Bible-chronology-charts-age-of-earth-date-Genesis-5-11-Septuagint-text-LXX-original-autograph-corrupted-Masoretic-MT-primeval-5554BC.htm).

138 Ibid.

139 David MacDonald, "The Flood: Mesopotamian Archaeological Evidence," National Centre for Science Education. Date of access: July 26, 2024 (https://ncse.ngo/flood-mesopotamian-archaeological-evidence).

140 Ibid.

141 Owen Jarus, "How Old Are the Egyptians Pyramids?" Live Science. August 29, 2023 (https://www.livescience.com/archaeology/ancient-egyptians/how-old-are-the-egyptian-pyramids).

142 "Entropy and the Second Law," Boston University. December 12, 1999 (https://physics.bu.edu/~duffy/py105/Secondlaw.html).

143 Jay Weatherill, "You don't get unity…" BrainyQuote. Date of access: August 8, 2024 (https://www.brainyquote.com/quotes/jay_weatherill_417602).

144 "On Truth & Reality," Space and Motion. Date of access: August 8, 2024 (https://www.spaceandmotion.com/Physics-Albert-Einstein-Theory-Relativity.htm).

145 Oliver Wendell Holmes Jr., "A goose flies by…" Goodreads. Date of access: August 8, 2024 (https://www.goodreads.com/author/quotes/432185.Oliver_Wendell_Holmes_Jr_?page=2).

146 "Archosaur," Britannica. Date of access: July 26, 2024 (https://www.britannica.com/animal/archosaur).

147 John P. Rafferty, "Did Dinosaurs Really Have Feathers?" Britannica. Date of access: July 26, 2024 (https://www.britannica.com/story/did-dinosaurs-really-have-feathers).

148 "Archosaur," Wikipedia. Date of access: July 26, 2024 (https://en.wikipedia.org/wiki/Archosaur).

149 Alfred Whitney Griswold, "The divine spark leaps…" BrainyQuote. Date of access: August 8, 2024 (https://www.brainyquote.com/quotes/alfred_whitney_griswold_408676).

150 "First Civilization in the World & Mesopotamia," Study.com. Date of access: August 8, 2024 (https://study.com/learn/lesson/video/mesopotamia-overview-civilization.html).

151 James T. Bartsch, "A Word Study of Tohu wa Bohu," WordExplain. Date of access: August 8, 2024 (https://www.wordexplain.com/Word_Study_tohu_wa_bohu.html).

152 Carl Rogers, "The facts are always friendly…" BrainyQuote. Date of access: August 8, 2024 (https://www.brainyquote.com/quotes/carl_rogers_147475).

153 "How Much Water Is There on Earth?" United States Geological Survey. November 13, 2019 (https://www.usgs.gov/special-topics/water-science-school/science/how-much-water-there-earth).

154 "Flaws in a Young-Earth Cooling Mechanism," National Center for Science Education. Date of access: August 8, 2024 (https://ncse.ngo/flaws-young-earth-cooling-mechanism).

155 Robert A. Moore, "The Impossible Voyage of Noah's Ark," National Center for Science Education. Date of access: July 26, 2024 (https://ncse.ngo/impossible-voyage-noahs-ark).

156 Ibid.

157 Wilmot H. Bradley, "The Varves and Climate of the Green River Epoch," United States Geological Survey. Date of access: July 26, 2024 (https://pubs.usgs.gov/pp/0158e/report.pdf).

158 Lorence Collins, "Twenty-One Reasons Noah's Worldwide Flood Never Happened," Northridge University. Date of access: July 26, 2024 (https://www.csun.edu/~vcgeo005/Nr38Reasons.pdf).

159 "Creation/Evolution," National Center for Science Education. Date of access: August 8, 2024 (https://ncse.ngo/files/pub/CEJ/pdfs/CEJ_01.pdf).

160 Michael Greshko, "What Are Mass Extinctions, and What Causes Them?" National Geographic. September 26, 2019 (https://www.nationalgeographic.com/science/article/mass-extinction).

161 Lorence Collins, "Twenty-One Reasons Noah's Worldwide Flood Never Happened," Northridge University. Date of access: July 26, 2024 (https://www.csun.edu/~vcgeo005/Nr38Reasons.pdf).

Milton Keynes UK
Ingram Content Group UK Ltd.
UKHW032034191024
449814UK00010B/535